Hell's Was

Black Squirrel Books™

an imprint of The Kent State University Press

Kent, Ohio 44242   www.KentStateUniversityPress.com

HELL'S
WASTELAND

The Pennsylvania Torso Murders

JAMES JESSEN BADAL

Frontis: A lonely stretch of deserted railroad track south of New Castle, Pennsylvania. The empty desolation of spots like this made them ideal dumping grounds for butchered murder victims. Photograph by Mark Wade Stone; courtesy of StoryWorks.TV.

BLACK SQUIRREL BOOKS™ 🐿™
Frisky, industrious black squirrels are a familiar sight on the Kent State University campus and the inspiration for Black Squirrel Books™, a trade imprint of The Kent State University Press. www.KentStateUniversityPress.com

Library of Congress Catalog Number 2012043494
ISBN 978-1-60635-153-6
Manufactured in the United States of America

Library of Congress Cataloging-in-Publication Data
Badal, James Jessen, 1943–
Hell's wasteland : the Pennsylvania torso murders / James Jessen Badal.
p. cm.
"Black squirrel books."
Includes bibliographical references and index.
ISBN 978-1-60635-153-6
1. Serial murders—Pennsylvania—New Castle.   2. Homicide investigation—Pennsylvania—New Castle.   3. Serial murders—Ohio—Cleveland.   4. Homicide investigation—Ohio—Cleveland.   I. Title.
HV6534.N38B33 2013
364.152'320974893—dc23
2012043494

17 16 15 14 13   5 4 3 2 1

For Paul, with deepest gratitude

"A puzzle inside a riddle wrapped in an enigma."

—*Winston Churchill on the Soviet Union*

CONTENTS

INTRODUCTION
AND ACKNOWLEDGMENTS

It's a story I have told many times. During the last two days of the semester in my eighth-grade American history class, our teacher, John Gillett, decided to regale us with the tale of Cleveland's infamous, unsolved torso murders from the mid-1930s, as told in John Bartlow Martin's article from the November 1949 issue of *Harper's Magazine*—a fascinating piece that bore the grimly alluring title "Butcher's Dozen: The Cleveland Torso Murders." Eighth grade was not exactly my finest hour as a student, but if my thirteen-year-old ears remained almost permanently deaf to the wonders of America's past, they certainly perked up as our teacher read Martin's vivid account of the brutal series of decapitation murders that pitted Cleveland's safety director, Eliot Ness, against the unseen and unidentified Butcher perpetrating horrible crimes in the central city, right under the noses of the police. I was fascinated, although as I eagerly soaked up the details of those unspeakable murder-dismemberments, the thought that I might one day write a book about this local fiend, dubbed by some city pundits "Cleveland's Jack the Ripper," never entered my mind. But write it I did. And when the Kent State University Press published *In the Wake of the Butcher: Cleveland's Torso Murders* in 2001, I thought that was the end of it: my long-standing debts to author John Bartlow Martin, to my American history teacher, John Gillett, and to the specters that still haunt Kingsbury Run had been paid.

In 2001, I certainly did not anticipate a second book on Cleveland's sensational butcheries. However, my nagging doubts about the "official" version of events, particularly concerning the arrest and death of Frank Dolezal, together with a sudden influx of information on that particular aspect of the case, led me to expand what had been a single chapter of *In the Wake of the Butcher* into a new book, *Though Murder Has No Tongue: The Lost Victim of Cleveland's Mad Butcher* (2010). The reasons behind this third book are a little more complex. In the midst of the cycle of murder-dismemberments going on in Cleveland came news from New Castle, Pennsylvania—a small industrial city southeast of Cleveland and north of Pittsburgh—that killings with remarkably similar modes of operation (MOs) had been going on there at least since the mid-1920s. Various officials from Cleveland made the relatively short trip to New Castle over the next couple of years to explore the possibility that all these grisly murders in both cities were somehow linked. Opinion was split: some cautiously hinted that there might be a connection, while others were more skeptical. Initially, the Cleveland press establishment gave scant attention to Pennsylvania's troubles. After all, local officials were divided about any possible link, and Cleveland was wrestling with its own ongoing nightmare of murder and mutilation. Decapitated and otherwise dismembered bodies had continued to appear at various points in the inner city despite the largest and most intense investigation in Cleveland history, and law enforcement seemed no closer to an answer than it had been when the killings officially began in September 1935. As far as the press was concerned, the Pennsylvania atrocities were an interesting footnote to the murder-dismemberments occurring in Cleveland. Although in my first book, *In the Wake of the Butcher,* I devoted some space to a discussion of the New Castle killings, I treated them as the local press had in the 1930s—as an intriguing sidelight to what was happening in Cleveland.

In 2003, Chuck Gove—an enterprising detective with an entrepreneurial flair in the Cleveland Police homicide unit—put together a three-hour bus tour with the catchy title of "Mystery, Mayhem, and Murder Tour," an odyssey that took Clevelanders with a yen for the city's dark past to all the sites and landmarks associated with the torso murders that had not been plowed under or built over, as well as to the Cuyahoga County Coroner's Office. The final attraction in this tour through the city's underbelly was the rather extensive and grisly display on the torso murders in the Cleveland Police Museum. When Gove inaugurated the tours, *In the Wake of the Butcher* had been gracing bookstore shelves for two years, and he asked me if I would meet the tour groups at the museum, sum up the entire case, and answer any questions. So, on specified Friday evenings for the last ten years—surrounded by old police photos of dismembered body parts and flanked by masks representing four of the victims—I've stood ready to answer any questions the mystery fans cared to ask. Invariably, there would be enquiries about "similar killings" going on outside Cleveland—specifically those pesky New Castle murders. Over time, I had crafted answers to such enquiries that ranged from noncommittal to dismissive. All of my responses tended to begin the same way: "Doubtful!" "Probably not!" "Hard to say!" "Can't be sure!"

It came to my attention, however, that other commentators who had written about the torso murders, either in book form or online, were nowhere near as reticent as I about connecting the Pennsylvania murders to those committed by Cleveland's Mad Butcher. In fact, some imaginative scribes seemed on the verge of attributing to a single perpetrator virtually every American murder occurring between 1925 and 1950 that involved decapitation, mutilation, or dismemberment. Such flights struck me as unnecessary attempts to puff up the reputation of Cleveland's Butcher to make his killings there more horrible and therefore, perhaps, more attractive to a modern true crime buff. In more recent years, after all, serial killers have operated over wide geographic areas and racked up impressively high body counts. Ted Bundy is thought to have thirty victims to his credit, while Gary Ridgway—the Green River Killer—killed close to fifty. Compared with these appalling statistics, the Butcher's officially recognized tally of twelve victims, spread out over four years and confined mostly to Cleveland's inner city, seems downright paltry. I suppose that in some writers' minds, expanding the size of the Butcher's hunting ground and granting him more victims were simply ways of giving him greater stature, of making him more "worthy" to stand alongside more recent and far more prolific serial killers. But Jack the Ripper is traditionally held responsible for only five vicious murders over a three-month period in the narrow confines of London's East End, and his stature in the history of serial murder is not diminished by either his low body count or the very small geographic area in which he operated. The Butcher's crimes rank among the most horrific imaginable, and assertions that he operated over an area far wider than inner-city Cleveland and racked up substantially more victims than he is traditionally blamed for do not make them more horrible.

The one clear, indisputable connection between the murders in the two cities, other than a certain similarity in their MOs, is Detective Peter Merylo of the Cleveland Police Department. A savvy professional sporting the department's best arrest record, he was assigned to the torso murders full time by the chief of police, George Matowitz, in early September 1936. By then, Cleveland's official body count stood at six, and events in the city had reached critical mass. The size and urgency of the police investigation into the unprecedented series of killings had been growing steadily since the cycle officially began in September 1935; the search for the killer was calling for ever-greater commitments of manpower from the beleaguered police department. City newspapers constantly ratcheted up the pressure, especially as it became clear that the police weren't getting anywhere in tracking down the perpetrator.

Beginning in August 1937, Merylo, the veteran detective, operated on the deeply held conviction that all the murder-dismemberments in both Cleveland and New Castle were the work of the same bloody perpetrator, and as time went on he based more and more of his investigative moves on this assumption. This belief also led him to employ some decidedly dangerous tactics; for example, he went underground, disguising himself as a transient and riding the rails linking Cleveland, New Castle, and Youngstown, mixing with society's down-and-outs — even eating and living with them — in a search for clues that would put him on the trail of the perpetrator. His assumption that all the murders were linked affected his assessment of potential suspects, leading him to give greater weight to those he judged physically capable of leading the arduous life of a hobo always on the move. Could this man mix easily with society's castoffs and gain their trust? Could he overpower his chosen victims?

It has become a pop culture cliché that for every cop there is that one special case that will consume him or her, and this notion receives constant reinforcement from *48 Hours Mystery, Dateline,* and a host of true crime dramas that depict a dedicated investigator still wrestling with a difficult cold case long after retirement. For Peter Merylo, that all-consuming case was the torso murders. For six years they possessed him, frustrated him, and ultimately defeated him. He slept badly, often lying awake mulling over stray bits of information and possible leads. Occasionally, he rose quietly from his bed, so as not to disturb his wife, and trudged out into the night for reasons only he understood.

He could turn distant and preoccupied at family gatherings. No one would say anything; perhaps family members pretended not to notice that the black clouds of Kingsbury Run had settled over him yet again.

Peter Merylo retired on March 15, 1943, ending his tenure as a Cleveland cop by submitting a hefty eleven-page, 3,500-word report on the case that haunted him. "I respectfully submit," it began, "the following report on the Torso Murders Investigation to which I was assigned from September 10, 1936 to October 1, 1942." In remarkably formal, dispassionate, and objective prose, the veteran cop laid out the course of the investigation that he and his partner, Martin Zalewski, had undertaken for six long and deeply frustrating years. It gave no hint of the sheer weariness or the mental turmoil that had burdened Merylo as he doggedly pursued one fruitless lead after another.

—

So, at the risk of being branded a true crime writer with a single arrow in his quiver labeled "Mad Butcher of Kingsbury Run," I decided to turn to the torso murders for a third time to explore those nagging questions about victims in western Pennsylvania apparently murdered in a fashion similar to the Cleveland victims—the last huge piece in the mammoth torso murder puzzle spanning three decades, covering two states, involving literally dozens of law enforcement professionals, and concerning more than two dozen victims murdered in the most gruesome manner imaginable. The Pennsylvania torso murders essentially break into three cycles: the first occurring in the early to mid-1920s; the second coming in 1925 and confined primarily to the area around New Castle that came to be known as Murder Swamp; and the third taking place roughly a decade later and culminating in the ghastly discoveries of May 3, 1940, in Stowe Township. I was somewhat surprised to find that no official documentation survives for the first or second series of murders—only the coverage in the local press. Moreover, major disagreements exist as to how many Pennsylvania victims there actually were; some sources put the body count as high as twenty. From where had these inflated totals come? When decapitation murders began in Cleveland in the mid-1930s, the city could boast of a reasonably professional police department (by the standards of the day), a duly elected coroner with a medical background, and a relatively well-equipped county morgue. In contrast, the resources existing in New Castle, Pennsylvania, and nearby towns when the murders there began more than a decade earlier were nowhere near that sophisticated. Procedural regulations among law enforcement officials were either nonexistent or far more casual in the small towns of western Pennsylvania than they were in Cleveland. Other than some notations in the sheriff's office, there were no police reports on the local killings in New Castle or the surrounding areas. In addition, there was no county morgue; dead bodies were taken to a local undertaking establishment and examined either by the undertaker or a physician, most likely a general practitioner lacking even the minimal forensic training available at the time. The post of coroner in that era was purely an elected bureaucratic position requiring no medical background or forensic experience. A coroner was essentially a paper shuffler who simply signed off on the conclusions arrived at by the undertaker or attending physician. There is, therefore, no official paper trail to follow for any of the Pennsylvania victims from the 1920s, a paucity of hard evidence that has resulted in a plethora of misinformation and confusion. The only contemporary accounts come from the newspapers of the day, leading to major disagreements among more recent writers as to the number of victims and the method used to decapitate them or otherwise mutilate their bodies. The resources available to researchers increased markedly with the third cycle of killings, beginning in the mid-1930s. By then, Cleveland's murderous Butcher had become embarrassing front-page news all over the country, so when murder victims seemingly decapitated or dismembered in a similar manner began turning up in dilapidated freight cars in Ohio-Pennsylvania railroad yards, the press coverage in the two-state area blossomed and the body of surviving official paperwork ballooned.

The biggest obstacle in researching the Pennsylvania murders was the almost total lack of any sort of official documentation covering the first and second series of killings during the 1920s. At the time, the New Castle press responded to the murders with extensive, detailed, front-page coverage; the viciousness of the crimes and the total mystery that surrounded them were virtually unprecedented. But any serious researcher quickly learns that newspaper stories must be treated with a healthy dose of caution. In the rush to meet deadlines and get out a sensational story ahead of the competition, journalists can confuse details and allow outright misinformation into their coverage. Fact and fancy stand side by side. It certainly helps if multiple papers covered the same event. In those cases, a researcher can check details in one publication against those in another, which may come from a second source. Also, in their coverage of an ongoing investigation, daily newspapers will often correct initial errors in their follow-up stories. Nevertheless, the dearth of official documentation on the first two series of killings does pose a problem. The official record is much more complete for the third set of Pennsylvania killings, during the 1930s; in fact, the triple horror of May 3, 1940, not only generated the widest and most intense newspaper coverage the torso murders had ever received but also spawned official affidavits, autopsy protocols, and police reports.

The largest repository of information on the Pennsylvania murders remains Peter Merylo's police reports and his memoirs. After leaving the Cleveland police force, he put in an abortive stint as chief of plant police at Tinnerman Products, had a brief flirtation with a State Department offer to work in Hawaii, and eventually opened his own detective agency. But the ghosts of Kingsbury Run silently followed him, hovering over him and apparently granting him little peace. Sometime after his retirement from the force, he tried to set the record straight on Kingsbury Run—and, perhaps, at the same time, to exorcise his personal demons—by writing his memoirs. The resulting manuscript of 155 8½-by-11-inch pages was seriously hobbled, however, by Merylo's stiffly formal, police-report writing style. He gave it another shot by collaborating with Frank Otwell, a friend who wrote for the *Cleveland News,* and the professional journalist's input clearly leavened the intimidating severity of Merylo's original prose.

—

Detective Harry Hanson of the Los Angeles Police Department used to refer to the scene of a murder as the "sacred setting." There was something almost mystical in his belief that the air of a crime scene vibrated with clues and an investigator need only be sensitive to them. I'm no Harry Hanson, but whenever I have bumped into one of those inevitable walls usually called "writer's block" while working on a book, I have invariably returnd to the scene of the crime or crimes I was researching. I so often walked down Linnet Avenue toward

Halloran Park and stood outside the modest house of Cleveland's most famous missing child, Beverly Potts, that I'm sure suspicious residents thought I was casing the neighborhood; I was obviously up to no good. Most of the sites related to the Kingsbury Run murders either have been irrevocably altered by progress or have completely disappeared—mowed down and covered over by modern highways or razed to make way for new construction. But whenever the words just would not come, I would visit the still-existing remnants of those horrible crime scenes or walk along the stretch of the Cuyahoga River where body parts floated by seventy years ago, hoping the ghosts or the muses would quietly whisper. (I had to be careful about going into Kingsbury Run proper. The land is now owned by the Cleveland Rapid Transit Authority, and RTA police will descend on anyone seen loitering there without official permission.)

One of the main reasons I had previously avoided writing about the Pennsylvania torso murders in any detail—in addition to the lack of surviving documentation and the division in contemporary informed opinion over whether they were related to the Cleveland murders— was that I did not know the area all that well. My paternal grandparents did live near Youngstown, and, thanks to a seven-year teaching stint in the western part of Pennsylvania, I was relatively familiar with New Castle and the surrounding environs. But my familiarity with the area was relatively shallow; I did not enjoy the same intimate connection to the Pennsylvania crime scenes that I had to those in Cleveland, and making a jaunt of some eighty-odd miles across the Ohio border to soak up the atmosphere whenever I hit a compositional snag hardly seemed practical. Then in October 2007 I received a manuscript in the mail: "Murder Swamp," written by Paul G. Johnson of Beaver Falls, Pennsylvania. He had meticulously researched the Pennsylvania butcheries, combing through old newspapers, city directories, and census records and even photographing what was left of the relevant crime scenes. He also speculated briefly about their possible connection to the atrocities in Cleveland. When I asked him if he had any intention of publishing his work, either in whole or in part, he replied, "No. I just enjoy researching the ghosts, not writing about them." By 2009, I had nearly completed work on *Though Murder Has No Tongue: The Lost Victim of Cleveland's Mad Butcher*. During the summer months, I was again down at the Cleveland Police Museum on specified Friday nights, answering questions from those who had taken Chuck Gove's torso murder tour, and, predictably, those enquiries about the Pennsylvania butcheries came up. Once having made the decision to look more closely at the murder-dismemberments in the Keystone State, I contacted Paul Johnson and asked for his help. Paul became my eyes and ears in western Pennsylvania. He drove me and TV producer Mark Wade Stone (a long-time collaborator) around the rural areas intimately connected to the murders; he showed us the Jackson property, the relevant railroad sidings, and the small piece of the notorious Murder Swamp that remains—even pointing out the exact spot where the angry search party of West Pittsburg and New Castle residents gathered on October 20, 1925, before entering the swamp in a determined, well-organized hunt for clues. He willingly shared the results of his research with me and gave me access to all the surviving official documents in his possession. Whenever I needed some local matters in Pennsylvania cleared up or simply checked, Paul became my trusted research arm. He also read through the sections of Peter Merylo's memoirs relating to the Pennsylvania killings and pointed out passages where the veteran cop's memory had played him false. Without Paul Johnson's wholehearted cooperation, this book could not exist in its present form, and I gratefully dedicate it to him.

Ever since the Kent State University Press (KSUP) published *In the Wake of the Butcher* in 2001, I have received a steady stream of e-mails either offering or seeking information about some aspect of Cleveland's most notorious case. In June 2011 I received a highly unusual—but undeniably intriguing—request from Luke Moussa, a graduate student studying geographic information systems technology at the University of Arizona and an intern with a behavioral analysis firm. The word *torso*, followed by those magic words I had heard and seen so many times in other enquiries over the past several years—"I have been bitten by the bug"—immediately grabbed my attention. Mr. Moussa was enlisting my cooperation for his final graduate project—a contemplated "geographical profile" of the torso murders in Cleveland. What little I knew about the geographic profiling of a series of crimes was derived from the concept of the "comfort zone"—a definable area of activity close to either the perpetrator's residence or another base of operation, the analysis of which will help lead to his or her arrest. During the investigation of the Kingsbury Run murders in Cleveland, law enforcement personnel had used a relatively primitive version of the technique. In a manner rather similar to the old-fashioned police practice of sticking pins in a map, local investigators had analyzed the pattern of dump sites and concluded that the killer lived either in or around Kingsbury Run. At the very least, he was familiar enough with the decaying industrial landscape and its shanty-town sprawl to move through the area quickly and with confidence. Many later investigative initiatives employed by the police or the office of the safety director, Eliot Ness, were based firmly on that assumption. The highly detailed study that Luke produced was so fascinating that I asked him if he would be willing to apply the same technique to the Pennsylvania murders. I'm happy to report that he readily agreed, and his analysis appears in the appendix of this book. Although KSUP and I gave considerable thought to including Luke's larger study of the Cleveland murders as well, we ultimately decided that doing so would be inappropriate in a book devoted primarily to the Pennsylvania killings. We did not want to omit it entirely, however, so interested readers will find Luke Moussa's complete analysis on the website of the KSUP.

Mark Wade Stone and I have been a research team for about ten years. His company, Storytellers Media Group, has produced Emmy Award–winning TV documentaries based on my books; and he has remained my valuable and trusted partner whether we were digging through archives at the Cuyahoga County Morgue, sorting through old press photos and newspaper clippings, interviewing potential sources, or just rehashing our discoveries over wine, soup, and salad. During the revisions phase of this book, I received a letter from Chris Starke, an English author and member of the Whitechapel Society (an organization devoted to the study of Jack the Ripper and his crimes), alerting me to a couple of murder-dismemberments from the early 1920s in the area of western Pennsylvania of which I had previously been unaware. While neither of these gruesome deaths could be attributed to Cleveland's Mad Butcher, they clearly demonstrate how wide the investigative net had been thrown at the time and how deeply problematic the investigation had become. Those murders have been added to this book, and I offer Chris my grateful thanks for bringing them to my attention.

Thanks also to Zachary L. Brodt, records manager at the University of Pittsburgh; Sam Mendez; Traci Nickerson, copy center, Cuyahoga Community College, Eastern Campus; and Will Rutherford, store repre-

sentative at the *Pittsburgh Post-Gazette*. I owe a considerable debt of gratitude to various individuals and committees at Cuyahoga Community
College for their constant support, especially my dean, Vince DiMaria.
As was the case with my previous books, my colleagues on the board
of trustees of the Cleveland Police Historical Society have been more
than generous with their support and encouragement. I also gratefully
acknowledge the cooperation of the Office of the Medical Examiner,
Allegheny County, Pennsylvania; the staff of Pennsylvania's Lawrence
County Historical Society; librarians in Special Collections at Cleveland
State University; and the staff of the photo archives department at the
Cleveland Plain Dealer. Finally, thanks to my old friend, artist Michael
Nevin, for producing drawings of Luigi Noschesi and James Nicholson
from terrible microfilm copies of old newspaper photographs.

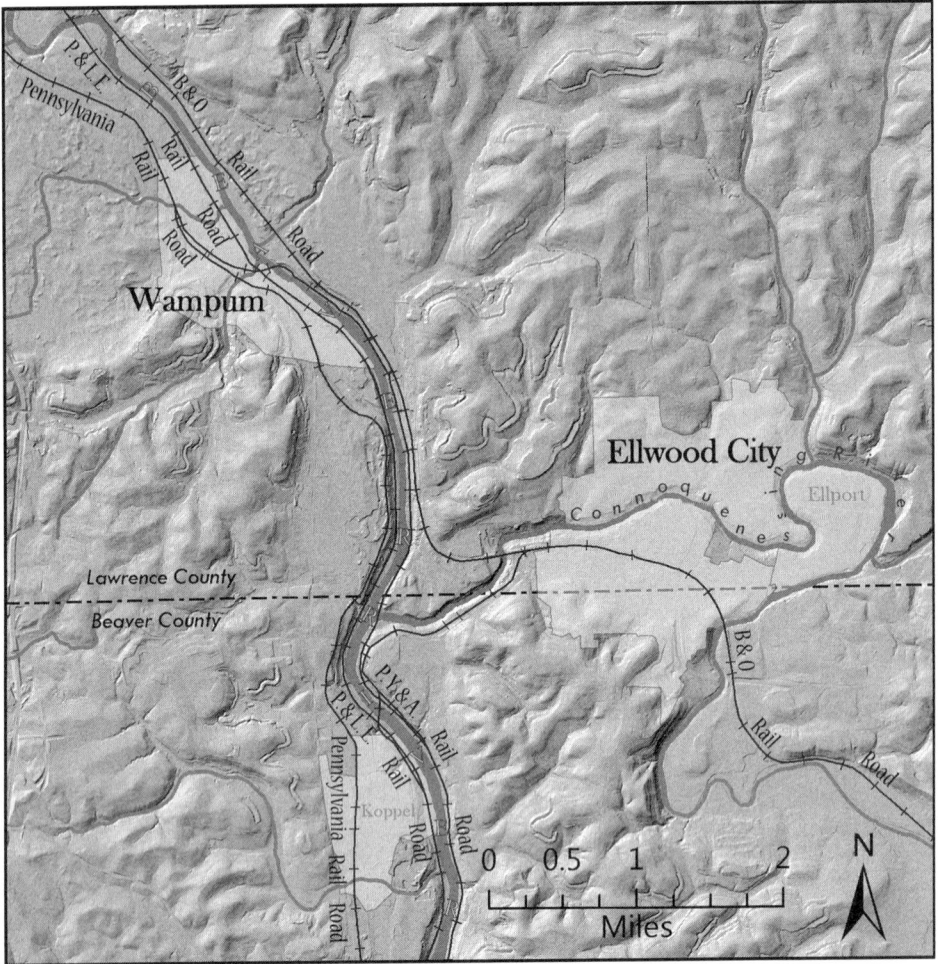

The area around Wampum, Pennsylvania, scene of Emma Jackson's murder. Map by Luke Moussa.

CHAPTER 1

MURDERS MOST FOUL

The morning of Wednesday, March 16, 1921, began like any other day on the Jackson family farm. Everything was utterly normal; all seemed as it should be. Achsa Jackson (whose admittedly odd first name was consistently misprinted by the New Castle press as "Ascha") had given her seventy-three-year-old mother Emma a parting kiss on the cheek as she left for her job as an instructor in the Ellwood City public schools. Her brother William had already gone to work at the National Tube Company, also in Ellwood City. The Jackson farm stood on Wampum Road, south of New Castle, Pennsylvania. The property had been in the family for thirty years; in fact, the Jacksons were known and respected in the rural area as one its "pioneer" families. On this particular morning, however, Emma Jackson was apprehensive. She told her daughter that earlier, at about 7:30, a short, stocky black man had turned up at the front door asking if some vacant buildings on the Jackson property were for rent. When Emma had informed him that they were not, the stranger had left—but something about him unnerved Emma. "He looked just like a fiend to me," she insisted to her daughter. At around 9:00 A.M., an identified witness watched curiously as a short, stocky black man left the Jackson property.

William Jackson arrived home from work a little before 4:00 P.M. and, after leaving his overcoat and dinner basket on the back porch, proceeded to putter in the yard. He heard someone banging on the front door; and when his mother failed to answer the noisy summons, William walked around to the front of the house where a neighbor boy, apparently on an errand, was still determinedly pounding on the door. William opened the unlocked door and peered into the empty house. "Mother! Mother!" he called several times, but no response broke the eerie silence. Could she be asleep? Perhaps she was ill, William wondered apprehensively. Or was she upstairs in her bedroom? As he neared the top of the stairs, he momentarily froze: there on the floor in front of him was a bloodstain. Now truly alarmed, he pushed his way into his mother's bedroom. In the waning afternoon sunlight, coupled with the flickering glow of a single lamp, he saw Emma Jackson lying across the bed, her head hanging over the edge. Her neck had been slashed—almost to the point of decapitation, according to later reports—and there was blood everywhere: all over the bed, soaked into the bedclothes, on his mother's face and neck, splattered on the wall, and pooling on the floor from the deep wound in her neck.

Soon after William's gruesome discovery, Charles Morrison, Ellwood City's acting chief of police, and Alexander Leslie, a former Lawrence County detective, arrived on the scene. They determined that Emma had been initially assaulted in the kitchen and then either chased or carried up the stairs by her assailant to the bedroom where her horrified son had discovered her body. Luridly dubbed by the *New Castle Herald* as "a fiend incarnate" and a "demon," the unknown perpetrator had viciously slashed Emma Jackson's throat from ear to ear, severing the jugular, with either a straight razor or a long-bladed knife. The attack must have occurred literally within minutes of Achsa Jackson's departure for work. Emma had done a huge load of laundry the day before, and the basket of damp clothes waiting to be ironed was still sitting where she had left it. Although the assailant had taken a small purse containing less than three dollars, robbery had apparently not been the motive; jewelry and other valuables in plain sight had not been touched. In a quaint combination of veiled innuendo and demure language—characteristic of a far more genteel age—the *New Castle Herald* hinted darkly at what the real motive behind the assault may have been. "The body was thrown across the bed in such a way and the old lady's clothes were found in such a position, that it is believed an intended criminal assault was planned on the aged woman."

Suspicion immediately fell on Joseph Thomas, a suspect in another murder committed several weeks before, that of Mrs. Anna Kirker of Mifflin Township in Allegheny County. The *New Castle Herald* branded Thomas as a "depraved negro," and initially the evidence, flimsy though

The B&O Railroad line passing by the Jackson family farm. Photograph by Mark Wade Stone; courtesy of StoryWorks.TV.

it may have been, seemed to support Thomas's involvement in Emma's murder. He matched the general description of the man who had come to the farm the morning of Emma's death, as well as those given for two other suspicious sightings of black men noticed near the Jackson property. In one, a black man had shown up at the Jacksons' door two days before the murder, begging food and coffee, and in the other, a black man of similar description had been spotted in a cave ominously close to the Jacksons' property. The day after Emma's death, Allegheny County detective James McGinley and Ellwood City's chief of police, C. J. Clarke, led state police on a thorough search of the underbrush and wooded areas surrounding the Jackson farm, but they found no new evidence nor any trace of the mysterious black man thought to be Joseph Thomas. Soon the spotlight moved away from Thomas; suspicion of his guilt in the Emma Jackson murder apparently evaporated as quickly as it had surfaced. At the coroner's inquest held on March 24, the jury returned a verdict of murder at the hands of an unknown assassin; police had obviously eliminated the elusive Joseph Thomas from consideration.

The brutal murder of Emma Jackson would never be solved, and lingering memories of its sheer horror would haunt the peaceful rural area for years. This was a crime of the big cities; acts this terrible and inexplicable just did not happen in the quiet farm lands of western Pennsylvania. The serpent had truly entered the Garden of Eden, and in the next couple of years, it would strike again with equally devastating viciousness.

—

On the evening of Tuesday, July 11, 1923, C. C. Whiteside, the manager of a stone quarry near Rock Point, Pennsylvania, was bathing with his son in the Beaver River just south of Wampum, where Emma Jackson had been murdered over two years earlier. Whiteside suddenly spotted something white near the shore, close to the roots of a tree, so, carrying a boat oar, he warily approached. When he carefully slid the oar under the putrid mass in an attempt to turn it over, he discovered that it was the torso of a young girl, approximately six years old: the head, arms, and legs were missing. The body had been in the water so long that the flesh sloughed off the back and ribs when Whiteside disturbed it.

The police were stymied. No child had been reported missing from the New Castle area in the last year, and there was simply no way to identify partial human remains so badly decomposed. Authorities surmised that the currents could have carried the torso down the Mahoning River from Youngstown, Ohio, or perhaps down the Shenango River from Sharon, Pennsylvania. No one was ever arrested for the crime; the unfortunate child was never identified; and the circumstances surrounding her terrible death would remain a total mystery.

—

The morning of October 3, 1923, began as another typical day for Stephen Cass, a mill worker in charge of a derrick along the Pittsburgh and Lake Erie Railroad in Pittsburgh's Southside. It was 9:45 A.M. "I had just walked down across the tracks behind a truck," Cass reported to the *Pittsburgh Press* later that day, "and sent the truck to Twenty-third St. along the [Monongahela] river for a load of stone when I wandered over to the shed used by girls for dressing for a swim [a municipal pool was close by]." Forbidden to smoke on the job, Cass—and likely other workers as well—drifted over to the shack when it was empty to light up and relax. "I stood in front of the shed for a few minutes before I looked in," Cass continued, "and when I did I think I must have been overcome by a dizziness." On the floor of the shed's dark interior lay the headless corpse of a relatively small man, naked except for its socks. Blood seemed to be everywhere, and what appeared to be bloody clothing had been thrown over the bare abdomen. Horrified by the appalling spectacle, Cass alerted a nearby watchman, called the police, and deliberately stayed away from the shack until authorities arrived. When responding police officers George Specht, W. Selbert, and George Reiff first canvassed the grisly crime scene, the terrible mystery only deepened. The victim's shabby clothes were freshly torn and bloody, indicating a fight, but there appeared to be no signs of a struggle in the shed's cramped, dark interior or on the body, itself, beyond the fact that one of the fists was tightly clenched. Even though houses stood close to the railroad tracks and the crime scene, no one had heard anything out of the ordinary, certainly nothing like a scream or a cry that would suggest a struggle. Residents insisted, however, that the thunder of passing locomotives would have drowned out any telltale sounds of violence. Most alarming of all, the severed head was missing. While one of the attending police officers rummaged through the pockets of the victim's coat in search of any clues to his identity, he found two photographs: one photo of three nurses with "Marian, Me, Bella S" hand printed at the top and a second photo of a nurse sitting in a rocking chair behind a hospital with "Thinking of You" inscribed at the top. Police also located bloody handprints on some railing that led to the water's edge, leading them to believe that the killer had gone down to the shore in the dark to wash the blood off his hands. As they were removing the body from the shack, police noticed a man spotted with bloodstains wandering by and immediately arrested him as a suspect. (He was subsequently identified as twenty-eight-year-old Nick Hoffman—a mentally unbalanced, homeless drifter—and was released.)

Within a couple of hours of Cass's grim discovery, three neighborhood boys were playing at the foot of 18th Street, where they found a piece of blood-soaked underwear. The trio followed a trail of blood that led away from the soiled undergarment toward a patch of rocks; and as they poked around in the blood-clotted debris with sticks, they unearthed a human head buried in the sand with several strands of hair sticking above the surface. The spot was only about one hundred feet away from the changing shed where the murder had apparently occurred. It isn't clear from either the newspaper coverage or the autopsy protocols whether the boys made their discovery while police were still on the crime scene; however, both body and head arrived at the morgue in time for the formal autopsy at 12:45 P.M.

Morgue superintendent John P. Black judged the victim to be twenty-five or twenty-six years old. The investigating officers at the scene of the crime thought that it looked as if the head had been removed with something sharp like a surgeon's knife, a conclusion borne out by Black's closer inspection. The work, however, had been noticeably sloppy; the knife had gotten stuck at one point and had to be twisted, thus leaving an extremely jagged incision. In the formal autopsy protocol, Dr. DeWayne G. Richey not only noted the uneven cuts and nicks on the head and trunk, he recorded a number of relatively superficial wounds, including five small lacerations over the bridge of the nose, on the head itself. Unfortunately, he did not indicate whether these injuries were fresh or old, so it is impossible to know if they were signs of a violent struggle immediately preceding death. There were no other distinguishing marks on the body save for a tattoo of a crescent on the back of the left hand, a dagger on the right arm, and a dagger plus a woman's head and some words the protocol describes as "peculiar hieroglyphic characters" on the other arm. Something about the appearance of the head, coupled with the "foreign" words tattooed on the left arm (that apparently no one could read), led police to surmise—incorrectly, as it turned out—that the victim was either Turkish or Arabian. The official cause of death was horrifying: "shock and hemorrhage following decapitation."

Almost immediately, ghoulish "official" theories about what may have happened to the unfortunate man began to swirl through the city, aided and abetted by the *Pittsburgh Post-Gazette*. Perhaps, he had been done in by the Black Hand—a violent gang of immigrant Italians (a precursor to the more highly organized mob) that operated a simple extortion racket. The organization had become especially violent during the preceding months, claiming at least one victim almost every week in the city. Or maybe a physician, surgeon, or medical student had murdered the unidentified man and spirited away the head for "psychopathic analysis." According to the local Pittsburgh daily, Captain of Detectives Louis Leff described the case as "one of the most mysterious and baffling murders within the annals of the detective bureau." Deputy Coroner John T. McQuaid reported that he could not remember another decapitation homicide in his twenty-five years of experience at the morgue, thus the sensational newspaper coverage surrounding such a gruesome killing caused a stampede of sorts at the local morgue. Residents, many of them young women according to the daily, gathered outside on October 5 for a chance to get glance at the body. There were so many people at the doors of the facility that McQuaid had trouble keeping order. People lined up triple file outside the morgue and passed by the corpse at an estimated rate of twenty a minute—an astonishing 10,000 morbidly curious Pittsburgh citizens. (Ironically, a similar sideshow carnival would erupt outside the Cuyahoga County Morgue in Cleveland when the body and head of that city's victim 4 were discovered in June 1936.)

Police investigative protocol in those days taught that murderers killed people they knew for simple reasons that anyone could understand, such as jealousy or greed. It was of paramount importance that a murder victim be identified as quickly as possible since that was recognized as one of the most important, if not the most decisive, step in apprehending the perpetrator. Pittsburgh police attention, therefore, immediately turned to the two photographs of the nurses retrieved from the victim's inside coat pocket. The investigation then moved with astonishing swiftness; and within a matter of days, police had come up with a number of possible identifications: William Boland (a one-time employee of Southside Hospital), Roy Lyle of Punxsutawney, and a man with the last name of McCarthy. None of these panned out, but by October 6, police established a positive identification—twenty-one-year-old Charles "Chuck" McGregor (obviously neither Turkish nor Arabian), a one-time automobile salesman from Kittanning, Pennsylvania. One of the pictured nurses—Inda West of Punxsutawney (most likely the "Me" in the photo of the three women)—had been tracked down to Philadelphia's Jefferson Hospital. Tearfully, she related she had sent at least one of the photos found with the body to McGregor while he was living in a Detroit hotel. Joseph McGregor of Clarion, Pennsylvania, brother of the dead man, confirmed the identification after police described the tattoos. In the formal "Proof of Identity," the victim's father, James, reported that his son Charles had originally been trained as a baker. He told the press that Charles was "of a roving disposition" and had joined the army after the armistice had been signed. He had not seen his son since October 1922. As detectives sifted through Charles McGregor's somewhat murky past, they learned that three years before his death, he had spent six months in prison for auto theft. In exchange for a lighter sentence, McGregor had apparently turned state's evidence against his accomplice, thus making revenge a probable motive for the killing.

The formal inquest was convened on November 28, 1923. The verdict was simple; there was little for the coroner's jury to do but echo the official cause of death recorded in the autopsy protocol and recommend that "the said Person or Persons [responsible for the crime] be apprehended and held to await the action of the grand jury upon a charge of Murder." A decidedly empty hope, as it turned out! There was no further progress in the investigation. No one was ever arrested for the terrible crime, but events in West Virginia four months later would propel the unfortunate Charles McGregor back into newspaper headlines.

—

Railroad workmen were emptying a freight car of cinders in the Scully Yards of the Pennsylvania Railroad in Weirton Junction, West Virginia, around 8:30 A.M. on a cold Monday morning, February 11, 1924, when they got a nasty, sickening surprise. As they laboriously shoveled out the huge load of cooling cinders, they saw a "large object" roll down one of the chutes. It turned out to be a badly burned male human head. Carefully sifting through the cinders, they uncovered a pair of arms and a pair of legs, also rather severely burned. Weirton police and authorities from both Hancock and Brooke counties appeared on the scene almost immediately. In spite of the burns, they thought the man looked Italian and placed his age at around thirty-five. A subsequent thorough search of over a dozen freight cars in the vicinity failed to turn up the missing torso. Obviously the uncovered body parts had been mixed in with or tossed into the cinders while they were still hot and smoldering; the flesh had quite literally cooked. Weirton stands directly west of Pittsburgh just across the state line. These particular freight cars had been loaded and shipped from Pennsylvania in mid-January and had been idling in the Scully Yards ever since. West Virginia authorities were, therefore, convinced the victim had been murdered, decapitated, and dismembered in the Keystone state. According to the *Pittsburgh Post-Gazette* on February 13, Coroner W. J. H. Walkinshaw in Wellsburg, West Virginia, dubbed the case the most "baffling ever called to the attention of Brooke County."

Contacted by West Virginia authorities via telegram, John Barry —head of the homicide division of the City Detective Bureau in Pittsburgh—began an organized search for reports of any missing locals. Initially, Pennsylvania authorities came up with three possible identifications: John H. Johnston, a forty-three-year-old general store operator from Brentwood who disappeared on January 20; Albert Rutoski, a laundry driver who simply vanished two weeks before while he was out making collections; or Fred J. Bezdek, an Etna tailor who vanished from his home on November 9 under extraordinarily strange circumstances. According to the *Pittsburgh Post-Gazette* of February 14, as guests gathered at the Bezdek family home for the bridal shower of his daughter Helen, Fred had abruptly announced to his youngest daughter that he was just going "down to the corner" and would be "right back." He never returned, and his family remained mystified by his inexplicable disappearance. Bezdek's son Cyril made the relatively short trip to the Wellsburg morgue in an attempt to identify the remains but was apparently unable to do so. Not only were the body parts badly scorched, but decomposition was progressing rapidly. The missing Albert Rutoski subsequently turned up very much alive in Pittsburgh, and the potential Johnson identification also failed to pan out. Workmen from the Scully Yards in Pittsburgh were actually transported en masse to Weirton Junction in the vain hope one of them would recognize the unfortunate victim. The mystery swirling around the still unidentified murder victim only deepened when Coroner Walkinshaw received a mysterious, anonymous phone call at his home. The caller was a man who promised to come into the morgue and identify the body, but he failed to make good on his promise. A curious disagreement arose between the coroner's office in West Virginia and the Pittsburgh police over the manner of death. Coroner Walkinshaw was inclined to believe that the victim was a transient who had tried to build a fire in the freight car and was accidently burned to death in the attempt—an extremely odd explanation, especially when there were no signs of the torso in the car and it looked as if the body parts had been separated from the trunk with an axe. Pittsburgh police firmly rejected such a tenuous hypothesis, insisting that it was a clear case of murder. Suddenly the specter of Charles McGregor, murdered and decapitated the previous October in Pittsburgh, rose ominously from the shadows. Because the cases seemed so similar and both men had been killed in Pittsburgh's Southside, Pittsburgh police reasoned that perhaps, the still unidentified victim found in West Virginia in February had been killed by McGregor's murderer to prevent him from revealing the killer's identity. These undeniably attractive conspiratorial musings received full play in the *Pittsburgh Post-Gazette* (though, oddly, in none of the other Pittsburgh papers), but there was no hard evidence to establish that link. In time, with no new leads to follow and no similar crimes to which they could be compared, the investigation simply petered out. The unfortunate Charles McGregor and the never-to-be-identified anonymous man of the cinders slowly faded from local memory.

—

It was not a particularly large fire; in fact, the burning shack was hardly noticeable as it flickered against the cold gray light of a January afternoon in a desolate area west of Ellwood City. Frank Black, an employee of the Pittsburgh and Lake Erie (P&LE) Railroad casually watched three boys silhouetted against the flames as they ran from the shack toward the tracks of the Baltimore and Ohio (B&O) Railroad. It was 12:35 P.M. Thursday, January 1, 1925, and as Black watched the small building collapse in on itself, he turned to some nearby railroad workmen. "Poor kids," he mused. "Their club is burning down." It hadn't been a very imposing structure—a makeshift hangout covered with corrugated metal in a ravine near the B&O Railroad Bridge and the Connoquenessing River, its builders a gang of boys in their early teens from Ellwood City who had christened themselves the Timber Wolves. Since the shack was doorless and windowless, the only access was through a hole in the roof approximately six feet from the ground. An iron stove served as the only comfort of home. The boys would gather there daily just to talk, hang out, and sometimes foment plans against a rival Ellwood City gang. This second gang, the Whip-Poor-Wills, had staked out its territory with a similar clubhouse further downriver on a hill near a stone quarry. It was a simple *Little Rascals* world, in which rambunctious kids would routinely stay out late—perhaps even all night. No one seemed to sense any danger, and as long as parents had a rough idea of where their children were and what they were doing, all was well.

On the evening of Wednesday, December 31, two of the Timber Wolves, gang leader Joe Statti and James Joseph, met at their primitive and not-so-secret haunt to celebrate the New Year in their own boyish fashion by huddling around the stove and cooking potatoes. They reportedly spent the entire chilly night in their shack and did not leave until 9:00 A.M., the morning of January 1. An hour later, fourteen-year-old Luigi Noschesi of Ellwood City bade his family a cheery farewell and went off to play with some friends. At around noon, Statti returned to the Timber Wolf shack, only to see it going up in flames. Sometime later, James Joseph and another Timber Wolf, Richard Means, joined him, and the three boys watched their clubhouse burn to the ground. When the fire died down, they rummaged dispiritedly through the wreckage to see if anything had survived the blaze. Under a piece of tin from the roof, they discovered a putrid mass of burned bones and flesh. As Statti stared at the revolting pile of tissue and bone, it gradually occurred to him that these remains could be human. But the other boys convinced him that it must be the body of a dog that had been unfortunate enough to get trapped in the structure as it burned, so after a short period of debate, the three boys buried the still-smoking mass and left. As the day drew to a close, Luigi Noschesi's parents began to wonder why the boy had not yet come home.

Days later, members of the New Castle press establishment would wonder how the three Timber Wolves could ever have thought the body they buried was that of a dog. The entrance to the shack was six feet above ground; how could a dog possibly have gotten in?

By the morning of Friday, January 2, the Noschesi family was frantic. Luigi had been gone for twenty-four hours, and a determined search by the missing boy's friends had come up empty. Amid the swirl of anxiety and excitement over the missing boy, reports about a clubhouse destroyed by fire and the body of a dead dog began to surface. Police went to the spot where the shack had stood and dug up what was clearly a fresh grave of some sort. When the authorities dug it up, the remains they unearthed did not resemble a dog but rather a human torso minus the head, arms, and legs. Was this the body of Luigi Noschesi? If so, what had happened to him? And where were the head and the extremities?

Police initially surmised that the missing pieces might be buried in the deep snow drifts surrounding the grave, but a thorough search turned up nothing. The first medical men—two from New Castle and two from Ellwood City—to study and dissect the mass tentatively judged the hip bones human, but couldn't be entirely sure. Suddenly, Joe Statti and James Joseph were picked up by Ellwood City police, grilled, and actually thrown into an Ellwood City jail. Shocked and tearful, they insisted they knew nothing about the remains they had uncovered in the debris of their destroyed clubhouse and even less about the Noschesi boy's disappearance.

On Monday, January 5, the remains were transported to the Mercy Hospital Pathological Bureau in Pittsburgh for further study; by noon the following day, a pathologist declared the bones to be those of a boy less than seventeen years of age. But those findings only deepened a mystery that the coroner, James. P. Caldwell, had already declared the most baffling case in his five-year career of service in Lawrence County. Though all the evidence, circumstantial at best, indicated that the torso was that of the missing Luigi Noschesi, the boy's parents clung to the notion that their son was still alive and steadfastly refused to accept the remains for burial. Moreover, the authorities were still mystified as to how the victim had died and how the torso had ended up in the burning shack. They quickly dismissed the notion that Noschesi had somehow gotten into the clubhouse and had lacked the strength to raise the door in the roof once the fire started. Such a scenario could not explain the missing limbs, and the fire, no matter how intense, could not have completely destroyed the skull. "Did some fiend in human form come

Fourteen-year-old Luigi Noschesi of Ellwood City, believed to have been a victim of murder and dismemberment in 1925. Drawing by Michael Nevin from a lost *New Castle News* photograph.

upon the Noschesi boy in the shack . . . foully murder him and then set fire to the shack in hope of destroying all traces of the lad?" asked the *New Castle News* on January 5. "Or is [it] that Luigi Noschesi ran away from home and the charred bones found in the smoldering embers of the shack Thursday afternoon, January 1, and buried by some of the boys, are those of some unfortunate dog or animal?"

For the first week of 1925, the poignant story of the missing boy and the gruesome tale of the charred remains dominated local newspapers. On Thursday, January 8, Coroner Caldwell convened an inquest that unfortunately did nothing to resolve the impenetrable mystery. Each member of the Timber Wolves that had been present during the burning of their clubhouse and its troubling aftermath testified separately before the jury, and since the significant details of all their stories matched, the panel judged that the boys were telling the truth. "We believe the body found in the ruins of the shack to be that of Luigi Noschesi," declared the inquest jury in its verdict. "We believe that Luigi Noschesi came to his death in the shack aforesaid sometime between 10:00 o'clock A. M. and 2:00 P. M., January 1, 1925," it continued. "From the testimony presented we can fix no responsibility for his death other than it was brought about by unknown persons." And there the intriguing saga of the burning clubhouse and its grisly contents ended. With his parents still desperately clinging to the belief that their son was alive somewhere, Luigi Noschesi passed from the headlines into a dimly remembered local legend. Other than the terrible death, itself, the most mystifying and frightening aspect of the entire horrible episode remains the speed with which everything occurred. Luigi Noschesi left his Ellwood City home around 10:00 A.M., while Joe Statti and James Joseph returned to their clubhouse about noon to find it in flames—an extraordinarily narrow window of opportunity. Sometime within that two-hour span, Luigi was murdered, dismembered, and decapitated, his killer either luring him into the Timber Wolves' shack or merely using it as a dump site. Other than the charred torso, none of the missing body parts would ever be recovered.

—

Although all five deaths involved decapitation or near-decapitation, it seems highly unlikely that the same individual who killed an elderly woman during an attempted sexual assault in Wampum, Pennsylvania, could also be responsible for the exceedingly vicious murder and mutilation of two children in the same general area—let alone two adult males in a different part of the state. (Both New Castle and Ellwood City lie in western Pennsylvania, to the northwest of Pittsburgh. New Castle, the larger of the two municipalities, is about fifty miles north of Pittsburgh, close to the Ohio border, while Ellwood City lies southwest of New Castle, about thirty miles above Pittsburgh. The area between the two cities is largely rural farmland.) Pennsylvania authorities were inclined to link the murder of Charles McGregor to the burned remains discovered in Weirton Junction, West Virginia, but that connection remains tenuous at best. It is conceivable—perhaps, even likely—that the unidentified six-year-old girl (1923) and Luigi Noschesi (1925) were dispatched and mutilated by the same vicious perpetrator. The crimes were committed in the same geographical area a mere eighteen months apart. Both victims were children, and the manners of dismemberment remained undeniably similar.

Over time, however, the specific details of the crimes would fade, blur, and run together in the public memory; and in succeeding years, a series of circumstances would coalesce and bind those five killings, not only to each other, but to additional cycles of murder and mutilation, one looming out of a deserted swampy area just south of New Castle, Pennsylvania, and the other from the blighted inner city neighborhoods of Cleveland, Ohio. All these crimes would come together in an expanding pattern of sickening brutality involving more than two dozen victims whose deaths were spread over almost three decades in a broad swath of western Pennsylvania and northeastern Ohio.

When naked, decapitated bodies began turning up in a putrid, swampy expanse just south of New Castle and east of the Beaver River in the mid-1920s, Pennsylvania authorities surmised that either warring bootleggers or elements of the mob operating in Youngstown, Ohio—eighteen miles east, just across the Pennsylvania state line— were using the desolate spot as a dumping ground for their victims. But then, during the 1930s, headless corpses and otherwise disarticulated remains began surfacing in Cleveland, Ohio—particularly in the rusted industrial areas near downtown and the debris-strewn gully known as Kingsbury Run. Police in both cities would ultimately find the haunting similarities among the MOs of these crimes intriguing and alarming.

Speculation about connections among them was bolstered by the existence of the railroad lines linking the industrial centers of New Castle and Cleveland like an iron nervous system; in fact, the B&O passed by the quiet farm where Emma Jackson had been murdered in 1921, as well as the sites where the torsos of the unidentified six-year-old girl and the teenaged boy thought to be Luigi Noschesi had turned up in 1923 and 1925, respectively. In Cleveland, those same lines ran through Kingsbury Run, passing abandoned factories and the numerous shanty towns that had sprung up because of the economic devastation of the Great Depression. Could the same exceedingly vicious perpetrator be operating in both cities? Perhaps the killer was a railroad employee or even a deranged transient, someone who mixed easily with society's dispossessed and used the iron rails as simple transportation—as a way of passing from one hunting ground to the next and as a handy escape route? A railroad worker or transient would also be familiar with the rail yards and the territory adjacent to them in both cities, the seedy areas surrounding the industrial landscapes. Such a predator would be able to move through these areas with confidence, picking up society's castoffs—ether in bars, flophouses, or on the streets—murdering them in the most brutal fashion imaginable, and dumping their disarticulated remains in isolated spots where the unwary would eventually discover them. To paraphrase Winston Churchill's famous cold war assessment of the Soviet Union, the murders were a series of perplexing mysteries wrapped in an impenetrable enigma.

NOTES

Very little official documentation of the first five Pennsylvania murders has survived. The information relevant to the 1921 murder of Emma Jackson is drawn from the *New Castle Herald*. That concerning the 1923 death of the un-identified six-year-old girl and the 1925 death of the teenaged boy thought to be Luigi Noschesi as well as the details of the burning of the Timber Wolves' clubhouse and its aftermath, is likewise drawn from newspaper accounts, in these cases from the *New Castle News*. The two Pittsburgh murders received full coverage in the *Pittsburgh Press,* the *Pittsburg Post-Gazette,* and the *New Castle News.* The coroner's verdict as to cause of death in the case of Charles McGregor is recorded in the autopsy protocol C-165–23. Additional infor-mation on the 1924 Weirton, West Virginia, killing appeared in two Ohio newspapers: the *East Liverpool Evening Review* and the *Steubenville Herald Star.*

Thanks to his extraordinarily varied career, James P. Caldwell, Lawrence County's coroner, remains one of the most interesting figures involved in the New Castle murders. Before his four terms in the coroner's office, he had been a newspaper reporter and editor. He ended his career by serving as treasurer and director of the Dollar Savings Association. Caldwell had no medical training. Autopsies were performed by local physicians or even undertakers. This regrettable state of affairs was apparently common in rural areas in the early decades of the twentieth century.

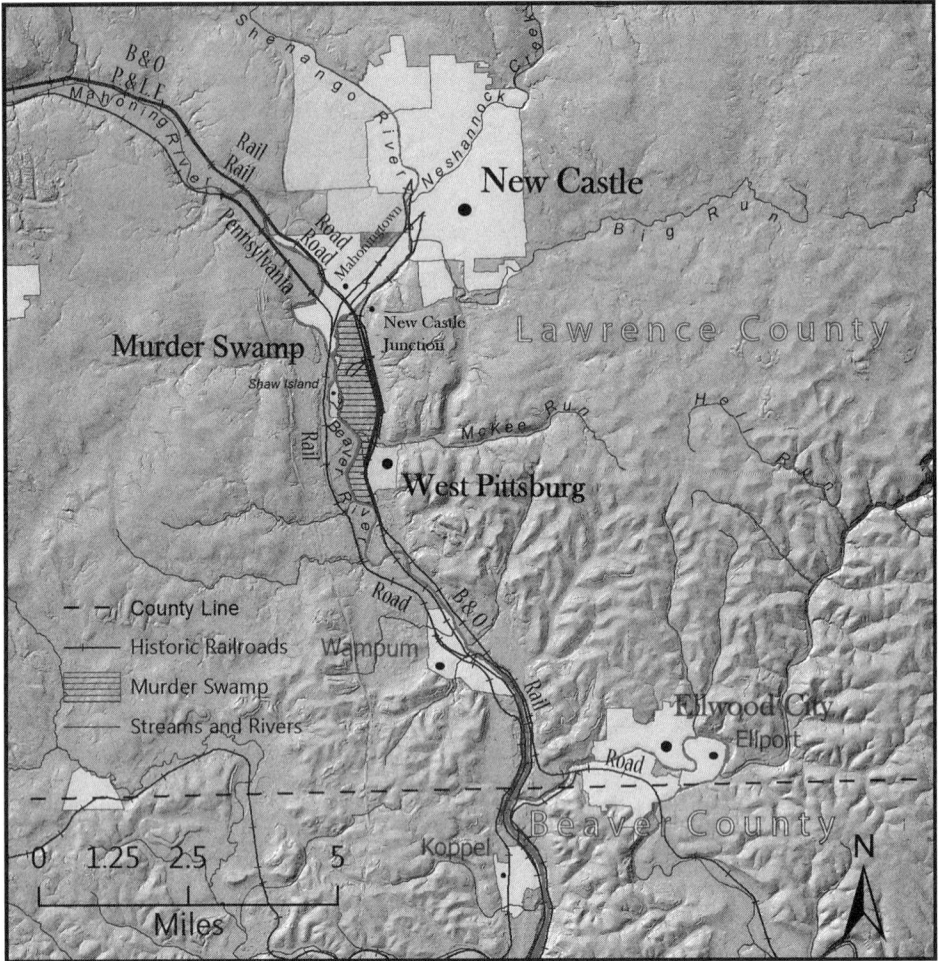

The New Castle and West Pittsburg region of Pennsylvania, showing the location of Murder Swamp. Map by Luke Moussa.

CHAPTER 2

THE TRIPLE MYSTERY OF 1925

New Castle, Pennsylvania, is a relatively small industrial city in the western part of the state, close to the Ohio border. Founded in 1798 by John Carlysle Stewart, the city became a part of the newly created Lawrence County in 1849. The construction of a canal system and the laying of railroad lines in the nineteenth century facilitated the easy transportation of raw materials and turned New Castle into a thriving industrial center of steel plants, paper mills, ceramic factories, and foundries. By the 1920s, the city had reached its zenith. Known as the tin plate capital of the world, New Castle was enjoying what would prove to be the peak of its economic prosperity.

But behind this optimism and growth festered a dark side. Since Lawrence County contained some of the most extensive limestone quarries in the world, the area attracted a substantial number of poor Italian immigrant stonecutters, looking for work and a better life in the United States. Beginning in the early 1900s, the criminal element of this immigrant population banded together to form a secret society that came to be known as the Black Hand, a less well-organized (though no less violent) precursor to the Mafia. The Black Hand's "business interests" were nowhere near as varied as those later developed by the Mafia; nor were their methods as sophisticated. The organization operated a simple extortion racket aimed at fleecing their better-heeled fellow immigrants. An intended target would receive a letter, decorated with a crude black hand, demanding money. If the individual did not pay up, he would be either beaten severely or actually killed. In 1907, the Black Hand murdered a local game warden, Sealey Houk, and an eighty-year-old farmer, "Squire" Duff—a double homicide that brought the full weight of New Castle's law enforcement establishment down on the organization in a sting operation that resulted in the arrest and trial of twenty-two defendants and the execution by hanging of gang leader Rocco Racco. Once Prohibition became the law of the land in 1920, illegal bootlegging, controlled by the mob, not only flourished but increased dramatically in Pittsburgh, Pennsylvania, and Youngstown, Ohio. Mob activity and power in both cities—as well as in Cleveland, Ohio—waxed and waned depending on the amount of civic and legal pressure brought to bear on illegal activities in those municipalities. It was a time of extraordinary violence. According to *Pittsburgh Post-Gazette* staff writer Torsten Ove, the territorial fights among various warring bootleg factions grew so fierce in western Pennsylvania that in the second half of the 1920s more than two hundred gangland murders and disappearances occurred in Allegheny County alone.

Directly south of New Castle, in Taylor Township, the Mahoning and Shenango rivers converge to form the Beaver River. Just east of this waterway, the B&O and the P&LE railroads snake forty-three miles south to McKees Rocks, Pennsylvania, and seventeen miles north to Youngstown, Ohio. The small community of West Pittsburg lies five miles southeast of New Castle. In between these landmarks lay a vast stretch of forbidding and largely impenetrable wasteland, composed of tangled undergrowth, blasted vegetation, dark woods, and putrid marsh that would soon develop a reputation for murder and mystery rivaling that of the English moors. The wasteland was a prime draw for area duck hunters and foragers of walnuts and fruits, and such locals knew of pathways leading into the dark interior of the marsh that were virtually undetectable to an outsider. Because of the blighted, isolated area's geographic proximity to Youngstown, the area would become the ideal dumping ground for the unfortunate victims of the ongoing bootlegging wars, eventually being dubbed Murder Swamp or Hell's Half Acre by the New Castle press. Little of the swamp remains today; part of the land has been reclaimed by the local power plant, and most of the marsh has simply been covered over with dirt. In the 1920s and 1930s, however, the vast waste cloaked an untold number of dark secrets; and they are still there—hidden by the power plant and buried beneath huge mounds of dirt.

A remote path leading into one of the few remaining stretches of the infamous Murder Swamp. Most of the area has been reclaimed, much of it by the local power plant. Photograph by Mark Wade Stone; courtesy of StoryWorks.TV.

—

The fog had not yet burned off, but the weather on Tuesday, October 6, 1925, was perfect for duck hunting. So thought thirty-three-year-old Samuel Hares of New Castle as he prowled the isolated expanse of swamp land and marsh close to West Pittsburg. Moving quietly, he had penetrated deep into its primeval hush and forbidding tangle of vegetation in search of ducks. Gradually, Hares became aware of a strange odor in the air, an oppressively foul smell that jolted him with a horrible sense of recognition. Twelve years before, while hunting in the same area, the smell of rotting flesh had led Hares to a badly decomposed body. Now that same putrid smell brought him to a large uprooted tree, where he glimpsed something sickeningly white, something that clearly did not belong there, protruding from beneath the fallen trunk. As Hares moved cautiously closer, he saw that it was the leg of a partially buried dead body. As quickly as possible, he returned to West Pittsburg, where he notified Walter Bannon, a constable of Taylor Township, of his gruesome find. Bannon was a Pennsylvania native, born in Moravia, who had worked on the Black Hand murders of 1907. Over the next dozen years, he would become one of the central figures in the investigation into the New Castle killings. Now accompanied by J. P. Caldwell, the coroner from New Castle, and county detective J. M. Dunlap, Bannon and Hares worked their way back through the marsh and underbrush to the spot where Hares had made his shocking discovery. It was a maddeningly slow and difficult slog, lasting more than an hour. When the group finally arrived at the isolated spot, the trio of authorities uncovered the naked corpse of a young man, reasonably well preserved except for being headless, which had been pushed into a sitting position in a deep depression under one of the upended roots and covered with a mixture of bark and twigs.

It was the sort of terrible discovery that takes the breath away, even from hardened cops used to dealing with the grime of society's underbelly; and in the stunned silence that followed, the men looked around in disbelief. The closest road that could support an automobile was more than two miles away, and there was no hint of broken vegetation in the area—nothing whatsoever to show that anyone had traversed the swampy ground carrying the dead weight of a human body to its lonely hiding place. And yet no other scenario seemed possible. Whoever the perpetrator was, he had exercised extraordinary care to ensure that the body would most likely never be found. "It was only by one chance in a thousand that anybody ever discovered the remains," mused Coroner Caldwell to the *New Castle News.* The four men poked around, pulling the underbrush aside in a search for the victim's head and clothes, but they found nothing. Whoever the murderer was, he obviously knew the forbidding territory well enough to navigate it with assurance and without difficulty, most likely at night. He had clearly taken elaborate pains to ensure that the victim would not be identified even if his body was found. Curiously, the killer had apparently returned to the disposal site recently and thrown more vegetation over the corpse; some of leaves were fresh and free of any sign of withering. It was, as the *New Castle News* proclaimed later that afternoon, "the most baffling murder mystery of many years in this county."

As the local daily informed its readers of the awful discovery in lurid detail, authorities made arrangements to have the body brought out of the swamp by wagon. It was an arduous process. The wagon could be driven only about a mile into the woods. The body had to be hand-carried out to that point. Finally, the corpse was transferred to an ambulance and driven to the Offutt Funeral Home in New Castle, where the remains were examined—not by a pathologist or anyone with medical training but by the undertakers, John C. and Frank B. Offutt. "It is the theory of Coroner Caldwell and County Detective Dunlap that the man was murdered somewhere else, and the body secreted for a time before being brought to the burial spot where the remains were found this morning," reported the *New Castle News*. The actual cause of death remained maddeningly elusive, however. There were no bullet holes or other detectable wounds on the headless corpse.

Law enforcement protocol in those days called for any dead body, whether of a murder victim or otherwise, to be identified as quickly as possible. This was partly a simple matter of respect for the dead; no one should be allowed to die anonymously or without the knowledge of loved ones. It was also a matter of established law enforcement wisdom, which held that a victim of murder in its various degrees was usually killed by someone he or she knew; hence, the first step in any murder investigation was identification of the victim. In this case, however, such identification seemed almost impossible; the corpse had no head, no scars or other distinctive marks, and no clothes. Moreover, the victim was decidedly average—a white male, between five feet eight inches and five feet ten inches tall and from twenty-five to forty-five years in age.

A few factors worked to the advantage of the authorities. For one thing, the body was in fairly good condition. Although the victim had been dead anywhere from two to four weeks, the damp, cold burial site, protected from the sunlight by the dark canopy of trees, had preserved the body. For another, even though the New Castle police had no official missing person reports on file, dozens of people seeking missing friends or relatives made enquiries. These seekers came from all over the surrounding area, including Ellwood City and Youngstown. Some wanted to see the body; others provided information about a loved one's former injuries, such as a broken bone or feet that had once been badly frostbitten, and asked that the corpse be reexamined for signs of such injuries. Neither the state of the body nor the information provided by members of the public led to an identification, however.

The local press had a field day speculating on exactly how the crime had been committed and the burial accomplished—whether more than one perpetrator had been involved, whether the burial had occurred during the day or at night, and from which direction the killer or killers had approached the burial site. "That the slayer possessed both nerve and cunning, [*sic*] is shown by the circumstances surrounding the case," declared the *New Castle News*. The daily also offered every motive imaginable for the crime, from a quarrel that got out of hand to robbery, from revenge to jealousy.

Around 3:00 P.M. on Thursday, October 8, authorities located the missing head, quite literally under their noses. Bannon, Dunlap, and others were conducting a more careful search of the discovery site when Detective C. W. Hicks noticed that the putrid smell hanging over the area was becoming stronger. When he poked under the fallen tree with a shovel, he unearthed the head, buried in a hole—apparently dug by hand—at the exact spot where the victim's feet had rested. Although the head was somewhat decomposed and filthy, authorities believed it was sufficiently well-preserved for identification. Seventy-five feet from the head, one of the searchers stumbled on a gray cap hidden in the bushes; then, forty feet from the cap, Detective Dunlap discovered evidence of a fairly large fire and the charred remains of two outer shirts. The initial supposition that the victim had been murdered elsewhere and the corpse carried to the deserted spot now gave way to the notion that he may have been killed, decapitated, and stripped on the spot where his body had been secreted. That would explain why the ashes from the fire contained the remnants of two shirts: one belonged to the murderer! His shirt had been bloodied when he removed the victim's head. But how had the killer managed to get his victim to this dismal spot? Had he been lured somehow? Had he been incapacitated in some manner and then brought here for some sort of execution? The discovery, about fifty feet from the remains of the fire, of five feet of sash cord knotted at one end seemed to support the latter theory.

Before taking the head to the Offutt Funeral Home for cleaning and further examination, Coroner Caldwell had New Castle photographer Clark Rutter take pictures of it in the hole where it lay; then, as darkness closed in, they placed the head on a box and lit it with automobile headlights so Rutter could take additional photographs. (There is an odd discrepancy here. On October 6, the newspapers had reported that the burial site was inaccessible by car, requiring police to carry the body a mile by hand to a wagon, which then transported it to a waiting ambulance. Was the head taken to another area to be photographed?) At the funeral home, the head was turned over to Dr. John Foster, who, since the newspapers did not name him as a specialist, probably was a general practitioner rather than a trained pathologist. Foster examined the head closely and determined that it had been severed from the trunk with a "very sharp instrument." (Given his probable lack of training, however, it is unclear how precise or sloppy the decapitation had been.) Once the head had been cleaned, authorities were able to report that the victim had long brown hair, a very good set of teeth with no fillings, and a "pug nose." Bruising over the left eye and temple led police to believe that he had been clubbed into unconsciousness before death. The head having been made more presentable—and recognizable—Rutter took additional photographs. Authorities were optimistic that the victim could now be identified. Although hundreds of people saw the photographs (the civic-minded photographer even posted a copy of the picture on the door of his studio), no identification was forthcoming. Unfortunately, none of these photographs have survived.

Coroner Caldwell ultimately made out a death certificate for an "Unknown Man" before the remains were quietly buried at Graceland Cemetery. Since there is no reason to believe that the spirit of yellow journalism was riding especially high in New Castle during the 1920s, the scope and intensity of the newspaper coverage of the crime indicate the depth of local horror; the case had shaken Lawrence County to its core. For three days, the disturbing story dominated the headlines and front pages of the *New Castle News*. "With no starting point, the case is one of the most baffling mysteries ever know in the county," proclaimed the daily on October 8. "In mystery and gruesomeness, the crime could scarcely be surpassed." Perhaps it would not be surpassed, but in the coming days, months, and years, it certainly would be more than equaled.

—

"West Pittsburg's dismal swamp, from which the headless victim of an assassin's knife was dragged on October 6, again gave up its dead Saturday evening when the skeleton of a second murdered man was carried from its gloomy depths." Thus the *New Castle News* alerted local residents to the discovery of another murder victim on Monday, October 19, 1925. Four young men from West Pittsburg—Charles Edmiston, John Wrangle, Tony O'Nick, and Andy Renser—had gone duck hunting in the swamp late on the afternoon of Saturday, October 17. Once within the marsh's gloomy interior, the group succumbed to the lure of mystery and decided to visit the infamous spot where the still-unidentified body of a young man had been discovered eleven days earlier. Leaving the trail, they struck out to the north through the unmarked tangle of vegetation, using their arms and hands to bat grasses, bushes, and tree limbs out of the way. Suddenly they saw something that looked like bone protruding from a clump of low bush. At first they thought it must be the remains of a dead animal. But the bones had been covered with a blue work shirt and an undershirt. When they pulled the remnants of clothing away, they saw what would later be identified as the skeleton, minus the skull, of a very large man. A pair of tan dress shoes had been dumped at one end, and a knife with a sharp but rusty four-inch blade lay nearby. Yet despite all this evidence, the men still were not sure that the skeleton was human.

Constable Walter Bannon also reacted skeptically when alerted to the admittedly suspicious find; but when he arrived at the discovery site and examined the bones, he had no doubt they were the remains of a human being, someone who had probably been dead since July or August. Bannon immediately telephoned Coroner Caldwell and Detective Dunlap, both veterans of the investigation into the body found on October 6. Word of the gruesome find spread quickly through West Pittsburg; and by the time the investigative team arrived on the scene, they were greeted by close to one hundred curious and apprehensive locals who had made the trek into the interior of the swamp. Remembering where the head of the first victim had been found, Caldwell asked the men to dig around and under the skeleton's feet. The work proceeded in grim silence, with only the slash and thud of shovels overturning dirt breaking the eerie quiet, but they found nothing. As night closed in, Caldwell produced two burlap bags: one for the bones, one for everything else. When authorities turned to leave the swamp, carrying their grim cargo slung over their shoulders, the onlookers marched silently behind them in single file out of the marsh toward the railroad tracks.

The remains were taken to the Offutt Funeral Home, where once again it was Dr. John Foster who presided over the examination.

Around noon on Monday, October 19, local excitement rose, only to turn into something resembling horror. D. C. Green and brothers Lew and Phillip Hawthorne had returned to the swamp, searching for anything that might help clear up the mystery of this second body. About two hundred yards from the original discovery site, the trio found a bundle of man's clothing. After Greene had left to report the find, the Hawthornes located a badly weathered skull—minus the lower jaw and several teeth from the upper jaw—partly hidden in the brush. Identification of the second body now seemed at least one step closer. But when Dr. Foster examined the new find, he dropped a bombshell. The skull did not belong to the male body taken from the swamp on Saturday; it was the skull of a woman who had been dead for close to a year! Amid an unnerving swirl of rumor and conjecture, involving false reports of murdered children and recent arrests, the alarmed residents of New Castle and West Pittsburg mobilized. "Spurred on by their eagerness to aid in the solution of the baffling triple mystery that confronts the authorities of Lawrence county [sic], and the entire community as well," trumpeted the *New Castle News* on October 20, "volunteers in considerable numbers answered the call of County Detective J. M. Dunlap, to assemble at West Pittsburg at noon today to start an organized search of the marsh." It was a scene straight out of an old Hollywood horror movie or western: angry villagers gathering with torches and pouring out on to the moors at night in search of the monster; indignant townsmen saddling up and joining the sheriff in a determined hunt for the cattle rustlers. (The *New Castle News* actually used the word *posse* to characterize this impromptu group of local would-be policemen.) Dressed in hunting garb, rubber hip boots, and any other heavy clothing that would protect against the dangers of the swamp, an eager crowd gathered at the south end of the marsh, near the Oil Works tank outside of West Pittsburg. Most carried long poles or clubs, anything they could use to knock the thick tangle of vegetation out of the way as they trudged into the interior. In those days, examination of a crime scene was a much more casual affair than it is today. Nothing was ever cordoned off; onlookers were allowed to wander at will; and using deputized civilians to aid in searches was not particularly unusual.

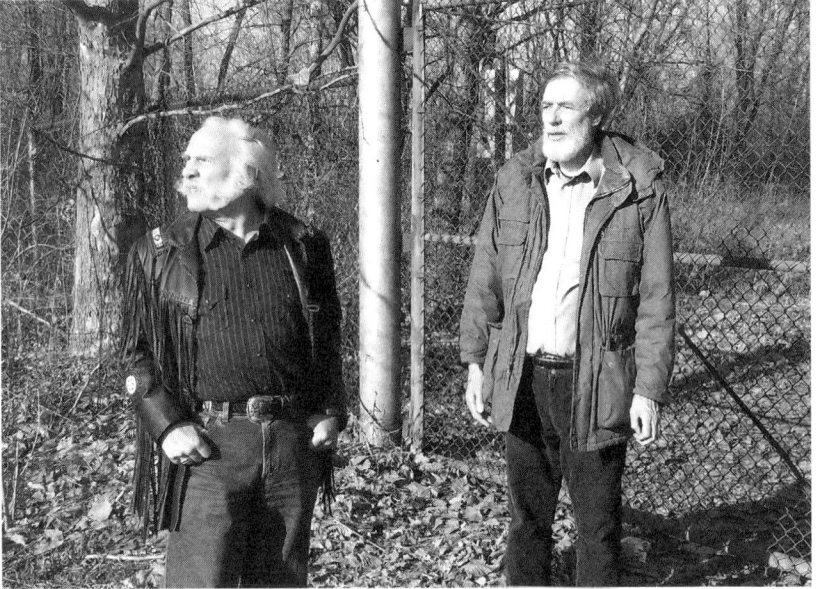

The author and researcher Paul Johnson on the spot where searchers gathered before spreading out into Murder Swamp on a determined hunt for clues. Photograph by Mark Wade Stone; courtesy of StoryWorks.TV.

Led by local authorities and state police from Butler, Pennsylvania, the large group spread out and moved systematically into the swamp. It is not entirely clear what they expected to find. The events of October, however, had made it abundantly clear that at least three dead bodies had been buried in the notorious marsh; how many more might there be hidden in its dark recesses? "How long this swamp has been used as a hiding place for murdered persons is only a matter of conjecture," cautioned the *New Castle News.* "Dozens of small pools dot the place, covered with green slime, and there is every possibility that the bottom of these may divulge some gruesome secret," hinted the local daily ominously. "Many of the bogs are little less than liquid and in these a body could be planted with little fear of disturbance." The searchers endured an arduous day-long trek over rutted ground that could trip a man and soft marsh that sucked at the boots, through tall grasses and reeds that had to be forced out of the way or cut down. Sometimes a fallen tree could serve as a handy bridge over a dangerous, slime-covered pool; sometimes that same tree could give way, plunging the unwary into the festering muck. A man couldn't even stand in the same place very long without shifting his position, for the ground could easily give way. Slowly, methodically, and with a grim determination worthy of Sherman's army marching through Georgia, the troops of volunteers worked their way through and over the treacherous landscape until descending darkness made the search dangerous, if not completely impossible.

The immediate results of this noon-to-night expedition were disappointing. The teams of searchers did recover a few more small bones — including the lower jaw of the skull unearthed the previous day — and some brown hairs, but these few bits and pieces of additional evidence were hardly enough to aid in the identification process. As a last resort, New Castle authorities had all the recovered clothing cleaned at a local dry cleaner and put on public display, hoping against hope that someone might recognize some of it. "Until this [identification] is established there does not appear to be any good starting point," worried the *New Castle News*. The organized search of the swamp area did have one totally unexpected and unwelcome consequence: it had generated so much publicity that similar but less well-organized rag-tag gangs stood ready to plunge into the area. Reluctantly, the authorities called off any additional forays until the publicity and excitement surrounding the first large-scale search died down. The well-publicized march through the swamp did accomplish one beneficial, long-term effect, however, although the jittery citizenry of New Castle and West Pittsburg would not recognize it for months or even years: all that activity obviously spooked someone. The marsh grew quiet, and the area did not yield up any more dead bodies.

As the trauma of the discoveries of October 1925 began to dissipate, a brief flurry of interest swirled around "Red" Fletcher, a former welder missing from Youngstown, Ohio, since September 23. He had reportedly told friends that he intended to go to New Castle, but he never arrived. Authorities could trace Fletcher's movements as far as the Liberty Road linking the two cities, but then the trail simply went cold. Could Fletcher be the first swamp victim, discovered on October 6? Police showed the photographs of the head recovered on October 8 to several of Fletcher's friends and associates, and though most stopped short of making a positive identification, one individual did say, according to the *New Castle*

News, "That's Red; all right." But even this promising development quickly evaporated when Fletcher's wife reported that he had written to her from Buffalo, New York, within the last week. Sheriff William G. Andrews, however, was apparently not buying it: he announced to the press that the search for Fletcher would go on until he was found alive. The results of that search are unknown. Whether the determined sheriff was ever able to locate the elusive Fletcher remains a mystery.

NOTES

The information relevant to the Black Hand, its history, and its activities is available on the website of the Lawrence County Historical Society: http://www.lawrencechs.com.

Torsten Ove's two-part article on mob history in Allegany County appeared in November 2000 in the *Pittsburgh Post-Gazette*. It can be accessed on the newspaper's website: http://www.post-gazette.com.

As indicated in the text, all the information about the 1925 Murder Swamp killings has been culled from the *New Castle News*.

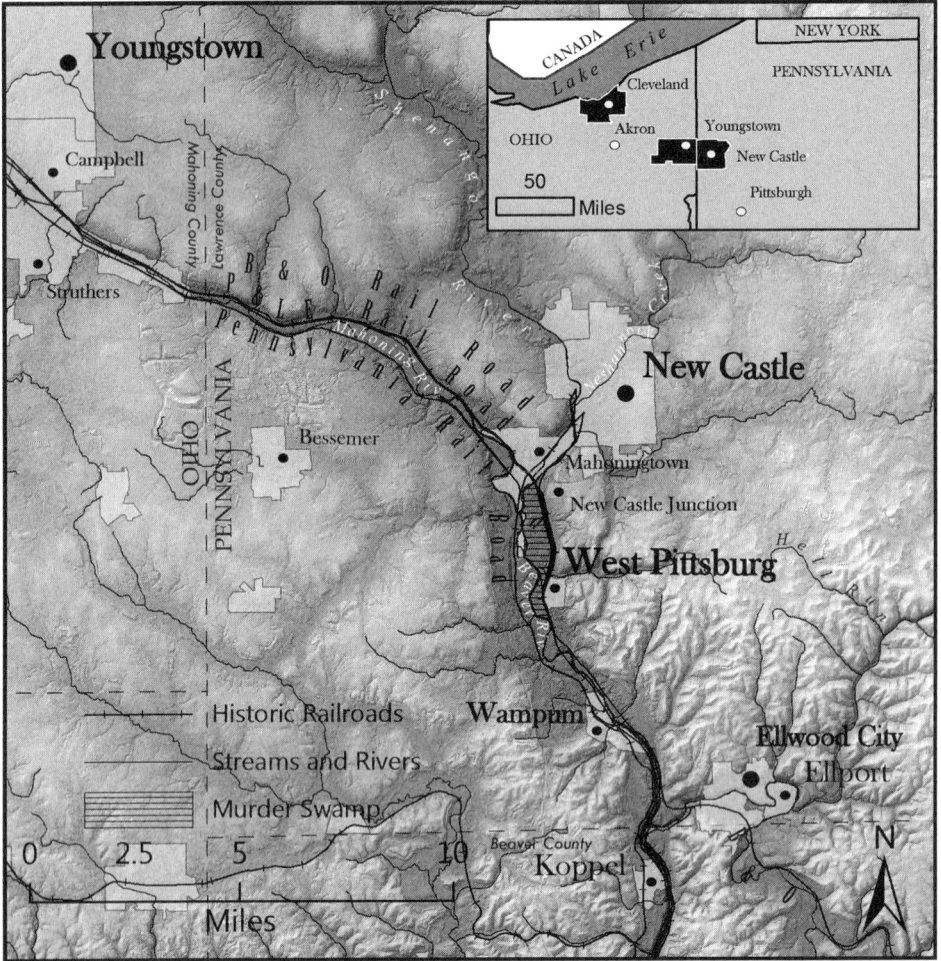

Region encompassing Cleveland and Youngstown, Ohio, and New Castle, Pennsylvania. Map by Luke Moussa.

CHAPTER 3

ENTER CLEVELAND

Just when the so-called torso murders began in Cleveland is a matter of debate. Some commentators fix the starting date at September 1934, when the rotting lower half of a woman's torso, thighs still attached, washed up on the shore of Lake Erie east of the city. Others opt for the more traditionally accepted date of September 23, 1935, when a couple of neighborhood boys discovered the naked, decapitated, and emasculated bodies of two men near East 55 at the base of a sixty-foot slope known locally as Jackass Hill. This shockingly gruesome pair of murder-mutilations would soon be followed by the similar decapitation-dismemberment of a woman in January 1936. By summer's end that year, six victims would be discovered—all decapitated and otherwise disarticulated by a knife-wielding phantom highly skilled at avoiding detection and possessing sufficient surgical skill to dispatch and further mutilate his victims with frightening precision. By the time the cycle of vicious murders stopped in August 1938, twelve officially recognized victims would be uncovered, the infamous "Butcher's Dozen."

The later months of 1936 were shaping up as an economically crucial period for Cleveland. Not only would the city play host to the Republican National Convention in June 1936 but the Great Lakes Exposition was slated to open at the end of June and run into October. City fathers desperately hoped these events would provide a financial shot in the arm for an industrial area still reeling from the devastation of the Great Depression. Given these hopes, the steady accumulation of decapitated and dismembered bodies was inconvenient, to say the least. Their discovery, just when Cleveland was counting on attracting free-spending

Cleveland's beleaguered safety director, Eliot Ness. By the summer of 1936, the torso murders in the city's Kingsbury Run area had become embarrassing national news, and Mayor Harold Burton ordered Ness to take a leading role in the hunt for the killer. When news of similar murders occurring in Pennsylvania reached the city, Ness dispatched his assistant, John R. Flynn, to New Castle to explore a possible link. Photograph courtesy of the Cleveland Public Library.

visitors to the city, alarmed Mayor Harold Burton, prompting him, apparently during the first week of September 1936, to meet with his hand-picked safety director, Eliot Ness, and his chief of police, George Matowitz. While Ness had been on the job since December 1935, initially he had given priority to cracking down on illegal gambling, labor racketeering, and corruption in the police department—"traditional" vices and crimes that would be comfortably familiar to a one-time G man. In a move that probably had as much to do with public relations as it did with investigative efficiency, Burton urged Ness to become far more directly involved in solving the torso murders than he had been up to that point. The mayor also ordered Chief Matowitz to assign his best man to the case full time. Thus Detective Peter Merylo picked up the threads of the baffling cycle of murder-dismemberments, and from his initial assignment until the investigation simply petered out, he and his partner, Martin Zalewski, became the public face of the torso murder investigation in Cleveland. They were first on the scene for each discovery, they served as point men for the whole police department, and they were the lawmen to whom the local press turned for updates and general comments. The torso murders would occupy Peter Merylo, indeed possess him, for the rest of his professional career and into his retirement.

Merylo immigrated to the United States from the Ukraine as a teen-ager sometime before the start of World War I. Although he joined the United States Army, he never saw any combat. When the war ended in 1919, he joined the Cleveland Police Department and rose steadily through the ranks, achieving that of detective in August 1931. On the job, he was often seen as a bewildering contradiction—a combination of a by-the-book team player and an independent maverick, willing to bend the rules if necessary to get the job done. He was a tenacious bulldog who pursued his assignments with an all-out dedication that would have exhausted his colleagues. Never shy about speaking his mind, he judged his brothers in the law enforcement fraternity by the extent of their determination and their records of competence. He liked and respected his chief, George Matowitz, but sparks flew when he had to deal with Eliot Ness, the dapper (and younger) safety director, who seemed at least as comfortable with the society set and newspa-per reporters as he did with his police officers. This friction between the two men would eventually have a huge impact on the manner in which the investigation was carried out.

—

It was Monday, October 15, 1934, and history was about to repeat itself. It had been nine years since the discoveries in Murder Swamp rocked the New Castle–West Pittsburg area, and since then, no further horrors had emerged from the infamous swamp. Now, however, all of that was about to change. Mike Seamans and A. J. Germani, two young men from West Pittsburg, had taken their dogs out for a good run about 5:00 in the evening. As the happy dogs raced and circled in an area a few feet from the Beaver River at the southwestern edge of the swamp, Seamans and Germani stumbled on the badly decomposed body of a six-foot-tall man with brown hair, lying facedown and partly covered by a thin layer of dirt. As the *New Castle News* proclaimed the next day, "another chapter was added to the gruesome mystery of the swamp." (The specific historical details begin to blur at this point. It had been nine years since the triple mystery of 1925, but the local daily asserted that the previous discoveries in the swamp had been made seven years before.) One of the more perplexing aspects of the new discovery was why no one had found the body sooner. Unlike the three secreted corpses of 1925, this body had been left at a spot where two rather heavily used paths converged, and there was ample evidence of recent foot traffic all over the area. Again, the reliable Constable Walter Bannon was the first official on the scene, and, since darkness was closing in quickly by the time he arrived, he and Coroner Orville Potter decided to leave the body alone until the next morning, at which time it was uncovered and transported to the Boyd Funeral Home for examination.

Determining identity and cause of death were the first orders of business, but both goals seemed unlikely, given the circumstances. West Pittsburg authorities had received no reports of anyone missing from the area in the last few months. Although police found a pint whiskey bottle and an iron spike of the sort used in highway construction under the head, there was nothing else—no clothes or any other articles that could aid in identification. The man had been dead for three months or longer, but there were no marks on the skull nor any indication that he had been shot or stabbed. (Significantly, he had not been decapitated, a fact that would later become crucial in any attempt to link his death to Cleveland's Mad Butcher.) The press assured its readers on October 18 that state and county officials were aggressively "still continuing their probe in the case," but conceded that "what meager clues are available do not seem to lead anywhere."

It is abundantly clear from the press coverage of this discovery that a belief that warring local mobsters in both Ohio and Pennsylvania were dumping their victims in the notorious swamp had taken firm hold in the nine years since the triple mystery of 1925. Reveling in the language of organized crime, the *New Castle News* referred darkly to "this illicit burying ground" and speculated openly about a "criminal gang" and unwanted persons being "taken for a ride." To a certain extent, this belief let New Castle and West Pittsburg police off the hook; murders committed in other jurisdictions, especially other states, were none of their business.

—

Railroad car repairmen E. B. Benn and A. C. Goodheart regularly inspected a string of twenty-three old boxcars that had been sitting abandoned for five years at a spot known as the New Castle Junction, near a slag dump of the P&LE Railroad. They had last examined the cars around June 10, 1936, but found nothing out of the ordinary, nothing to cause alarm or prompt a closer inspection. The doors of all the cars were kept closed but probably weren't secure; the doors of derelict boxcars were usually fastened with bent nails that could be easily removed. About two weeks later, on July 1, the pair walked the line again; a nearby resident, Oscar Wukovich had noticed hawks circling suspiciously above the abandoned cars and alerted authorities. And, indeed, this time something was wrong. The door on one car stood open, and as Benn and Goodheart approached to heave the large, bulky door shut, they recoiled from a putrid odor emanating from the car's interior. When they checked inside, they were greeted by the sickening spectacle of a headless, badly decomposed corpse of what looked like a man, covered with a burlap bag. The head was nowhere to be found—neither within the boxcar nor in the surrounding area. They alerted Sheriff Edward D. Pritchard of Lawrence County, who immediately arrived at the New Castle Junction accompanied by an impressively large contingent of law enforcement personnel, including a state policeman, a county detective, and Coroner Orville Potter.

Battling the oppressive heat and the horrible stench of the boxcar's claustrophobic interior, the assembled lawmen struggled to make sense of the grisly scene. When they carefully lifted the corpse, they uncovered one Cleveland and two Pittsburgh newspapers, dating from July 1933—all stained with blood—and a partly filled sack of cigarette tobacco. The body was in such deplorable condition that determining identity was impossible; it was even difficult to discern the race of the victim. In the immediate aftermath of the discovery, both local newspapers and Sheriff Prichard himself indulged in some really far-fetched theories about the actions of the killer or killers and the timing of the murder. The *New Castle News* actually suggested that the dates on the newspapers found with the corpse might indicate when the murder took place, a highly unlikely theory considering the papers were three years old and the body—though in an advanced state of decomposition—was hardly skeletal. For his part, Pritchard suggested that the murderer or murderers had returned to the boxcar after leaving the body there, to check if anyone had found their handiwork—a ludicrous theory that reduces the perpetrators from vicious killers coldly disposing of a dead body to immature and rather ghoulish teenagers waiting gleefully in the shadows to see if the sight of their carefully planted mess was having the desired effect on whoever discovered it. It just made no sense. Why would anyone who could kill so brutally care whether the body was found?

—

New Castle's triple mystery of 1925 seems to have remained a strictly local affair; no news of the Murder Swamp victims ever reached Cleveland. The later discoveries of the mid-thirties, however—the body found in the swamp in 1934 and the one found in the boxcar along the railroad lines in 1936—changed all that. Cleveland's law enforcement community first learned of the murders in western Pennsylvania sometime in late 1936 or very early 1937. Interestingly, the alert came from local newspaper men, not the New Castle police. Authorities in Pennsylvania certainly must have known about the murders in Cleveland; the crimes had become embarrassing national news. By then, the official body count in Cleveland stood at six, and, despite what was shaping up to be the largest investigation in city history, local police seemed no closer to an arrest than they had when the savage cycle had begun more than a year before. The possibility that Cleveland's Mad Butcher was also active in the Keystone State seemed likely to complicate an already difficult investigation enormously. When the news from Pennsylvania arrived, John R. Flynn, assistant to Cleveland's safety director, Eliot Ness, drove with an unidentified ranking officer from the Cleveland Police Department to New Castle, where Lawrence County officials briefed them and gave them a tour of the infamous Murder Swamp. (There is some confusion here. In one version of his memoirs, Detective Merylo does not identify this second man. In an alternate version, Merylo insists that the man was actually Eliot Ness, which seems unlikely. Yet in his final police report, submitted upon his retirement in March 1943, Merylo asserts that the man was James Hogan of the homicide division. See the notes at the end of this chapter for a full discussion of Merylo's memoirs.) Regardless of whether the famous Eliot Ness was present, Flynn, as Ness's representative, was given the red-carpet treatment by Lawrence County officialdom. Sheriff Pritchard, New Castle's chief of police, R. A. Criswell, and Lieutenant George S. Kennedy served as his guides. Flynn also spoke with Goodheart and Benn, the two P&LE inspectors who had discovered the fifth officially recognized New Castle victim on July 1, 1936, in a deserted boxcar.

To Flynn's dismay, he learned that, except for some brief notations in a record book at the sheriff's office, no official paperwork survived on the three Pennsylvania victims killed in the mid-1920s. This lack of paperwork should not be taken as a sign of laxity or laziness on the part of Pennsylvania authorities. The New Castle police force of that period lacked the personnel, forensic training, and resources of its Cleveland counterpart. Moreover, since no missing person reports from the New Castle area came to light at the time of the killings, the police ultimately concluded that the victims were casualties of the Youngstown, Ohio, bootleg wars whose bodies had been dumped in their backyard. Hence, there was little local police could do, especially as they had other cases far more pressing and important than sorting out the gangland murders of a neighboring state. This assumption that the Murder Swamp bodies were victims of out-of-state bootleg wars also explains why New Castle police did not contact their counterparts in Cleveland when the torso murders began; they simply saw no connection between what they believed were victims of mob violence and the unidentified unfortunates dispatched and mutilated by a psychopath for his own inexplicable reasons.

New Castle officials had retained so little evidence on the 1920s Murder Swamp investigation that when Flynn and his associate returned to Cleveland, they had precious little they could tell their chief of police, Matowitz. "Flynn returned to Cleveland a little dubious about the New Castle torsos," Merylo remarked in his unpublished memoirs. "He wasn't sure those murders had been committed by the same man responsible for those bodies here." Merylo, however, bluntly disagreed. "I was sure. I was so sure—and still am sure—that I volunteered to spend my next furlough in New Castle. And what I learned then—and since—have [sic] convinced me the murders were committed by the same man." From where did this unshakable assurance come? Unfortunately,

Detective Peter Merylo, the face of the torso murder investigation in Cleveland. Merylo was assigned to the Kingsbury Run murders by Cleveland's chief of police, George Matowitz, in September 1936. He traveled repeatedly to New Castle, Pittsburgh, and Youngstown between 1938 and 1940 and never wavered in his conviction that all the torso murders in the Ohio-Pennsylvania area were connected. Photograph courtesy of the Cleveland Public Library.

the veteran cop does not specify in any detail why he was so convinced of a connection in the face of the doubts expressed by the men who first went to New Castle from Cleveland and conferred with Lawrence County officials, but when Merylo began checking on the freight lines connecting the two metropolitan areas, that assurance only hardened and deepened. From this point on, western Pennsylvania always hovered in the back of Peter Merylo's mind, even as he and his partner, Martin Zalewski, pursued leads of their own in Cleveland and its backyard.

—

The portrait of Merylo that has come down in the lore of Kingsbury Run is complex. No one doubted his skill as an investigator or his dedication to the job, but the word *obsessed* occurs frequently in his contemporaries' assessment of him. Where does dedication end and obsession begin? Where is the line to be drawn? And can personal obsession become so strong that the investigator loses sight of possibilities that fall outside the scope of his focus? Merylo's unshakable conviction that all the murder-dismemberments in both locales were linked not only shaped the direction of his investigation but also determined the kind of suspects he would seriously consider. In his mind, a viable suspect had to be the sort of man who could ride the rails between Cleveland and New Castle, mix easily with the transient populations that gathered in the hobo jungles of both cities, and gain their trust while avoiding suspicion.

In his memoirs, Merylo recalls that he drove his wife and two daughters to New Castle in July 1937 for the sole purpose of showing them Murder Swamp—an area his spouse judged "very spooky" even in broad daylight. After returning his family to Cleveland, he drove back to Pennsylvania and spent the remainder of his two-week vacation familiarizing himself with the Murder Swamp killings, talking to the locals, and pursuing leads on his own. (Contrary to Merylo's recollection, in his memoirs, that this sojourn occurred in July, it most likely took place in August. See the notes at the end of this chapter for clarification of this admittedly minor point.) Constable Bannon, the seasoned veteran of all the New Castle slayings, served as Merylo's principle contact and guide. Bannon must not have worn his years very well; although he was in his fifties at the time, Merylo thought he was in his seventies. Merylo dug more deeply into the killings than John Flynn had done. Flynn had met with New Castle officials and toured the swamp. Merylo not only canvassed the area where the bodies had been found, he also ferreted out and talked with those residents who lived near the swamp. Merylo's thoroughness didn't help much, though. Most of the Murder Swamp victims had been dispatched more than a decade before his visit, and although locals' memories of the horrific discoveries remained startlingly vivid, the specific details had blurred over the years. Merylo returned to Cleveland with a number of misconceptions about the Pennsylvania murders. He assumed that all the victims were male and had been decapitated, but the third victim was female, and the body of the fourth victim was intact. Merylo also reported that there had been twelve victims when at this point in time only five bodies had been recovered. Even if those of Emma Jackson and the two children, found in the early 1920s, are added, the tally of Pennsylvania dead known by August 1937 still falls short of a dozen. How did Merylo come up with this inflated figure? It is extremely unlikely that Walter Bannon, a major player in the investigations of all the Murder Swamp victims, was sufficiently irresponsible to give the Cleveland detective such an inaccurate figure.

However flawed his information, Merylo remained convinced that the murders in Pennsylvania and those in and around Cleveland were linked.

> After collecting all the data in New Castle, and unable to uncover an new clew that would lead to the solution of these crimes, I returned home and immediately reported to Chief Matowitz' Office where I advised the Chief that I was convinced beyond any doubt that the murders in New Castle were identically the same as they were in Cleveland, and that I felt that the killer uses the box cars to dissect the body. I believed that the same individual who committed the murders in New Castle also committed the murders in Cleveland and I also believed that the killer rides a freight train.

This statement from his memoirs may reflect the conviction that Merylo ultimately developed, years later, about the nature of the per-petrator, but it is highly doubtful he was this sure about some of the details immediately after his first visit to New Castle in 1937. At this time—July or perhaps August of that year—the only body that could be definitely linked to a freight car was the badly decomposed corpse of the fifth officially recognized New Castle victim, found on July 1, 1936. The four previous victims—three found in the 1920s and the fourth in 1934—had all turned up in Murder Swamp. It would certainly seem, therefore, that Merylo's insistence in his memoirs that he had realized in 1937 that the killer rode the rails and accomplished his butcheries in a boxcar was not accurate. A savvy cop like Merylo would not have made that kind of investigative assumption based on a single case out of five. Later Pennsylvania victims (the sixth found in October 1939, as well as the seventh, eighth, and ninth found in May 1940) would be discovered in boxcars; hence, Merylo's belief about the role of freight cars in the killings probably should be dated from this later period rather than from August 1937.

By late 1940 or early 1941, Merylo's theories about the nature of the Pennsylvania killings were fully developed. In his memoirs, however, whether intentionally or not, he seems to be redirecting his matured notions about the case from the early 1940s back to August 1937. This obvious backdating may also explain his inflated estimate of a dozen Pennsylvania victims by 1936–37. In 1937, only five official victims had been found, and by 1940, there would, indeed, be very close to a dozen. Even though Merylo's memoirs were never published, the mistaken notion that Pennsylvania had twelve related victims by 1936 or 1937 would pass into torso murder lore as an undisputed fact. In his November 1949 article in *Harper's Magazine,* John Bartlow Martin wrote, "Now, in October 1936, the Cleveland police received word from New Castle, Pennsylvania, that some thirteen nude, headless bodies had been found near there in the past ten years." In his July 1952 piece in *Front Page Detective,* Paul McClung gave a similar tally when he described Merylo's activities directly after having been assigned to the Kingsbury Run murders in September 1936. "He studied the dozen torso murders that had occurred in the New Castle swamp along the railroad right-of-way in Pennsylvania." Some more recent sources have inflated the figure to as high as twenty victims, all of them killed after the murders in Cleveland stopped in August 1938.

—

For the second time since the triple mystery of 1925, Murder Swamp grew quiet and slumbered. But, as he pushed his investigation forward in Cleveland, Merylo always kept his eye on western Pennsylvania and its notorious swamp. It would be another two years before the next eruption of violence in the Keystone state, but when the evidence surfaced, it would be found along the railroad lines—not in the swamp—and it would rival anything that had transpired in Cleveland—or, for that matter, earlier in Pennsylvania—for sheer viciousness and horror.

NOTES

At his death in 1958, Peter Merylo left behind two different typed manuscripts of memoirs, neither of which was ever published. The longer of the two, at 156 pages, is clearly his own work; the style is as stilted and officially formal as his police reports. The shorter and far more readable manuscript of 107 pages was coauthored by a close friend of Merylo's, *Cleveland News* reporter Frank Otwell. There is no way to specifically date either set of memoirs, although both were probably written after his retirement in 1943. Unfortunately, there is also no way to be certain which of the two manuscripts came first, although it would seem likely that Otwell offered his services to his friend when he saw how bland Merylo's first attempts at autobiography and history actually were.

These memoirs contain a number of errors, especially when Merylo is writing about events in which he was not directly involved—although most of them are minor mistakes of chronology and dating. His assertion that he first went to New Castle in July 1937 is a case in point. Since his official police reports detail his investigation in Cleveland throughout that July, it remains extremely doubtful whether his first unofficial visit to New Castle could have taken place when he says it did. There are no surviving local reports, however, from the later weeks of August. It is far more likely he made his trip to New Castle at that time.

CHAPTER 4

THE DARKEST CIRCLES OF HELL

Ben Grinder, a switchman for the P&LE Railroad, reported for work along the rail lines near West Pittsburg at 3:35 P.M. on September 29, 1939. Sometime between 10:00 and 11:00 P.M., he noticed something glimmering in the coal-black darkness, and he glanced toward the edge of the notorious Murder Swamp less than two hundred yards away. He watched with casual interest as a small fire flared up, burned, and then suddenly flickered out. A hobo bonfire, perhaps—but why did it die so quickly? A few days later, car inspector George (Paddy) McCart and pump station worker Jim Carroll watched curiously as crows circled and clustered in the same general area where Grinder had first noticed the fire. Bird sightings over the swamp were not unusual, but there was something strange about this particular gathering of noisy crows.

Any New Castle or West Pittsburg residents with long memories must have come to dread the month of October. Not only had the 1925 discovery of three bodies and the subsequent march through Murder Swamp taken place during that month, but the 1934 discovery of another body in the same general area had also occurred in October. Now during the same month—on Friday, October 13, 1939, to be exact—three young men left West Pittsburg with nothing more serious on their minds than gathering walnuts, only to find that this Friday the 13th would live up to its grim reputation. At about 3:30 in the afternoon, Robert Durning, Carl Kos, and William Kessler were searching for nuts about a mile north of West Pittsburg along the edge of Murder Swamp when they made an exceptionally ghastly discovery—the headless, naked, decaying body of what seemed to be a young man, lying on its chest over

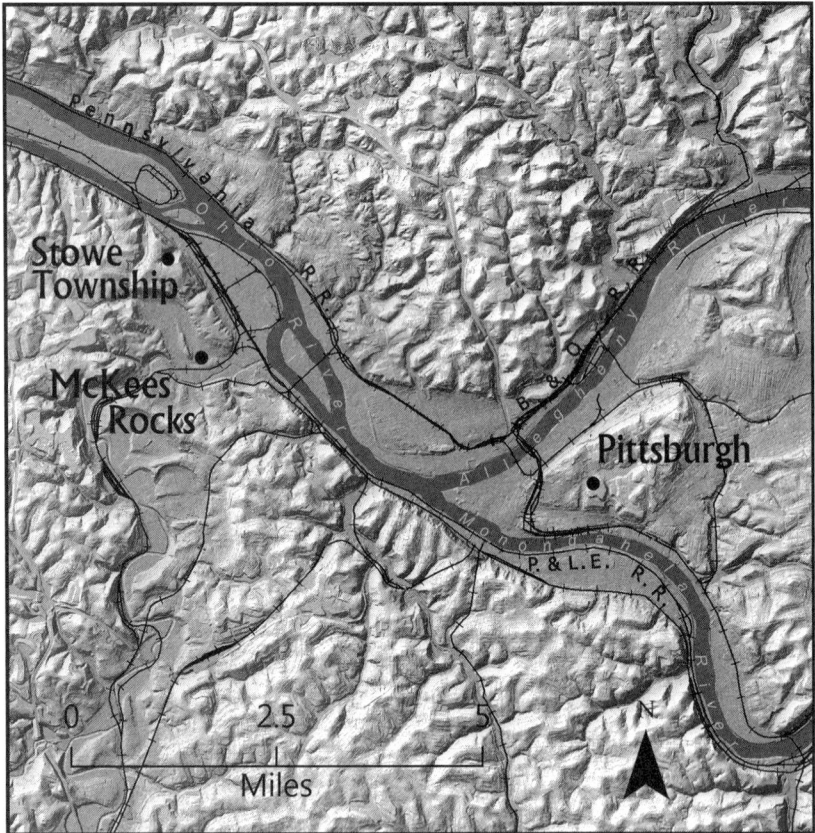

Region encompassing Stowe Township, McKees Rocks, and Pittsburgh, Pennsylvania. Map by Luke Moussa.

the remains of a fire. Obviously, someone had done his best to destroy the corpse by burning it with newspapers and gasoline or, at the very least, to frustrate any attempts at identification. To foil any attempt to lift fingerprints, the fingers had been burned by placing paper in the clutched hands and then igniting it. As the boys headed for a nearby gas station to phone authorities, they chanced to meet Merle Papa, a railroad employee and neighbor of young Kos, who, after hearing of the boys' grim find, notified Walter Bannon. The constable immediately headed for the scene, along with the coroner, Charles P. Byers, two state patrolmen, and three deputy sheriffs. The coroner examined the cut that had removed the victim's head, but was unable to determine whether it had been made by a large knife, a saw, or maybe even an axe. As the assembled lawmen combed the area for clues, the body was transported to the Leyde Mortuary in New Castle, where Dr. David Perry determined that the victim—a young man five feet, six inches tall, weighing 120 pounds and being about eighteen or nineteen years of age—had been dead for about two weeks, a conclusion subsequently borne out by the discovery of a newspaper on the scene—the September 28 edition of the *Youngstown Vindicator*. When the body finally arrived at the morgue, Perry tried unsuccessfully to get a set of useable fingerprints from the charred hands. As with all the previous victims found in Murder Swamp, clues were few and frustrations quickly mounted. No local reports had been filed of missing persons, and the few pieces of recovered evidence (an ankle bracelet, a pair of shoes, a partly burned blue work shirt collar, and some pieces of heavy paper) were of no help in identifying the body.

Ever since Eliot Ness's assistant John R. Flynn had first visited New Castle in late 1936 or early 1937 in order to learn more about the Murder Swamp killings, Cleveland's law enforcement fraternity had kept a watchful eye on events in western Pennsylvania. Local authorities may not have shared Detective Peter Merylo's unshakable conviction that Cleveland's Mad Butcher was also responsible for the atrocities, but they were wary: some of the details surrounding the earlier Pennsylvania murders had borne just enough resemblance to the local killings to keep lingering suspicions alive. So when Constable Bannon alerted Merylo by phone of the latest discovery (which he described as "something pretty good"), the veteran detective, together with his partner, Martin Zalewski; David Cowles, head of Cleveland's Scientific Identification Bureau (SIB); and Cowles's assistant, Lloyd Trunk, were on the road to New Castle by the afternoon of Saturday, October 14. While Corporal William H. Brush briefed the Cleveland contingent at the Pennsylvania State Troopers Headquarters in New Castle, West Pittsburg authorities were trudging around the swamp near the discovery site, looking for the still-missing head. At the Leyde Mortuary, Lloyd Trunk photographed the corpse from various angles (evidence that has since vanished) while David Cowles removed some vertebrae from the neck for microscopic examination—the only sure method of determining whether or not the decapitation had been accomplished with a knife. Merylo closely examined the "putrid carcass," later noting in his memoirs that "the man had small hands and feet, well-polished nails, [and] small bones."

Step by step, the investigations in Pennsylvania and Cleveland were becoming a joint effort. The local district attorney, John G. Larmoree, met with the Cleveland contingent and promised the full cooperation of his office. Since there were undeniable similarities among the murder-dismemberments in both states, it is not unreasonable to speculate that all the killings were related. The Butcher had not killed in Cleveland since August 1938; perhaps, he had pulled up stakes and shifted his activities to Pennsylvania. That was certainly Peter Merylo's position; he confidently told the *New Castle News* that he was convinced this most recent killing was the work of Cleveland's Butcher, adding, "I believe too that the slayer is a pervert." David Cowles was far more circumspect, refusing to speak with the press until the results of his tests were available. In his official report, apparently submitted the next day, Merylo again underscored his belief that the Mad Butcher of Kingsbury Run was now running amok in Pennsylvania. "From our investigation," he asserted, "we are of the opinion that the body of the nude man which was found in the outskirts of New Castle, Pa. tallies with our torso murders in Kingsbury Run." As the four lawmen from Cleveland headed home, the Pennsylvania state motor police were planning an organized search for the head in Murder Swamp—a virtual reenactment of the massive march through the same area in 1925.

—

It was Thursday, October 19, six days had passed since the three boys made their horrific discovery at the edge of the swamp, and the missing head still had not been found. Two days earlier, the *New Castle News* had reflected somewhat somberly, "There was a lull today in the investigation of the West Pittsburg murder of a man whose headless torso was found by youthful walnut-seekers at 3:30 P.M. Friday." But that was about to change. George McCart, the railroad car inspector, walked along a line of such train cars that had been moved, around October 8, from the east yard to the canal track—a spot only seven hundred feet from the swampy area where the three young men had discovered the headless corpse on October 13. As he passed a gondola of the Pittsburgh, McKeesport, and Youghiogheny (PMcK&Y) Railroad, McCart suddenly noticed a strange, sickening odor that seemed to come from the car itself. He climbed up and peered inside. The vile odor was stronger, much stronger. As he scanned the rusted interior, he noticed, in the empty first hopper, a heap of leaves that looked suspiciously as if they had been piled into one of the corners. Lowering himself to the floor, McCart cautiously approached the mass of debris; the odor was now overwhelming. Beneath the scattered leaves and twigs, he saw a partly decomposed human head with sandy-colored hair.

The state motor police, the sheriff's office, county detectives, the district attorney, and the coroner responded immediately to word of the grisly find. Initially, they assumed that the head had been jammed into the corner and then purposefully concealed with leaves, but after carefully examining the site, they abandoned that theory. There were blood stains in the area where the head lay, suggesting that the perpetrator had either dropped it from the top of the car or even tossed it like a basketball from the ground over the gondola's edge, allowing it to roll to its resting place, collecting leaves and bits of debris on the way. There were burrs stuck in the rather longish, matted hair, probably picked up as the murderer walked through the underbrush, carrying his ghastly trophy from the spot where the body had been burned to the empty gondola.

The new discovery brought the same four Cleveland officials to the scene the same day—Detectives Merylo and Zalewski, together with Cowles and Trunk. In the meantime, local personnel had photographed the head at the Lyde Mortuary, and District Attorney Lamoree and Coroner Byers had decided to have a Moulage cast made, a process that would produce a life-like plastic mask that could be instrumental in the identification process. (None of these artifacts have survived.) After a meeting between the officials from both states, the Cleveland contingent—accompanied by Bannon and Lamoree, and the Pennsylvania state motor police—visited both the site where the body had been found and the gondola that had contained the head.

At the original discovery site in the swamp, Merylo detected caked blood under some leaves and indications that blood had also soaked into the ground (although he couldn't tell how deeply), all of which suggested that the young victim had been at least decapitated, if not actually killed, on the spot where his body had been found. When Merylo examined the gondola closely, he found some small hairs that, according to his report of October 21, "no doubt came from around the region of the penis of the body." (He unfortunately does not speculate how the victim's pubic hair wound up with his head.) The detective also managed to find additional human hairs that subsequent tests determined did belong to the victim, as well as two teeth that apparently had been knocked loose when the head tumbled to its resting place at the bottom of the car. (The evidence envelope containing those teeth, and bearing Merylo's signature, is part of the collection at the Cleveland Police Historical Society Museum.) Ever the thorough cop (and a bit of a loner), Merylo returned to the railroad yard alone the next day and scoured the area for additional clues. He spoke with some of the railroad men, who told him that the features of the head resembled those of an effeminate blond man they had seen hanging around the yard about a month before. He had dressed like a man but walked like a woman; some of the men even thought he might have been a hermaphrodite. A traveling carnival had been playing a series of one-night stands nearby, and they wondered if the strange figure might have been tied to it somehow. Unfortunately, Merylo's subsequent attempts to track the carnival came up empty. Apparently too small to attract much notice, it had pulled up stakes and moved on after a single day's residence.

The discovery of the head, together with further talks with Constable Bannon, only deepened Merylo's conviction that Cleveland's Mad Butcher had, indeed, deserted his former hunting grounds on the Lake Erie shore to prowl the lonely railroad yards and dismal swamps of western Pennsylvania. "He [Bannon] was able to tell us enough [about the previous Pennsylvania victims] to convince us beyond a shadow of a doubt, all the headless victims found in that locality [Murder Swamp] had been murdered by the Cleveland's [*sic*] butcher. Bannon himself agreed, and so did the District Attorney, County Detectives and Pennsylvania State Police," Merylo declares in his memoirs.

Merylo's use of the word *us* was a tad misleading. As head of the Scientific Identification Bureau, Cowles was was nowhere near as certain that the murders in Cleveland and in western Pennsylvania were connected, and was tight-lipped about such a potential link. For one thing, preliminary tests indicated that the head had been removed with a saw, rather than with an axe or a knife. The Mad Butcher of Kingsbury Run had never used a saw. It is also unclear exactly how much Pennsylvania authorities knew about the murder-dismemberments in neighboring Ohio. Were they really that sure of a connection, or was Merylo simply marshalling their tentative agreement to firm up his own case?

Sometime during this period of hectic activity, Merylo talked with *New Castle News* reporter Edward H. Fritz. Although he was primarily a sports writer with a particular fondness for boxing, Fritz had also managed to cover several of New Castle's more sensational murder cases, including the Murder Swamp killings. "[He] informed me on the quiet," Merylo wrote in his two-page report of October 21, "that he believed he had a definite suspect who may be responsible for all the torso murders in New Castle as well as in this city [Cleveland]." Fritz then somewhat inaccurately described the 1921 murder of Emma Jackson in Wampum, Pennsylvania, incorrectly insisting that she had been completely decapitated by her unidentified attacker. The Jackson murder was eighteen years old in 1939. Memories over time become blurred; legends grow from dimly remembered facts. The initial reports of Emma Jackson's murder noted that her throat had been slashed; they made no mention of decapitation. Fritz, recalled Merylo, "stated that at that time he had information that a man who was thought to be one-half colored and one-half Mexican had entered this home and killed this woman but the investigation more or less collapsed at the time and no arrests were made." Moreover, Merylo continued, Fritz "also stated . . . that he received information that this murderer was working then and still is on this railroad." Fritz's description of the alleged killer is interesting, but his revelations never led to anything concrete. Had it not been for Merylo's report of October 21, this significant conversation—eighteen years after the fact—would have been lost to history. Such is the role of chance in human affairs! This brief conversation clearly explains why Merylo believed so strongly that the Mad Butcher was a railroad man and why he insisted in later years that the New Castle killings began in the early 1920s, not with the swamp murders of 1925.

—

It was May 3, 1940, and the horrible events of this day, rivaling the most lurid pulp novel, would leave railroad workers deeply shaken, veteran lawmen stunned, and morgue personnel shaking their heads in disbelief. Harry F. Gross, a foreman for the P&LE Railroad, and LeRoy Rust, a scrap inspector, walked idly along a string of nineteen derelict freight cars that had been brought to the company reclamation plant in Stowe Township, Pennsylvania, for demolition. The old abandoned boxcars had arrived at the east yard in McKees Rocks, Pennsylvania, from Struthers, Ohio, on April 21. On May 2, the string had been moved to the reclamation plant in Stowe Township for dismantling. It was 9:15 A.M., and Gross and Rust were giving each car a final check for occupancy or any other irregularity before it was scrapped. It was not unusual to find such cars occupied. Thanks to its double-floor construction and weatherproofed, reinforced side walls, even the most dilapidated boxcar guaranteed better protection from the brutal weather conditions than a bonfire. Assuming he were warmly dressed, all a resident would need to sleep in relative comfort, even in the coldest weather, would be some old newspapers to serve as mattress and blankets. Gross approached car 80179 and removed the bent nail that held the door closed. As he pushed the door aside to look in the interior, he suddenly recoiled from the sickening stench coming from the car. Peering into the darkness, he saw something that resembled the body of a dead dog, with a burlap bag lying beside it, in a corner of the car. When he entered the gloomy enclosure for a closer look, he realized it was a nude human torso, minus the head, arms, and legs; the missing limbs were subsequently found in the burlap bag. Gross immediately reported his grisly discovery to his supervisor, N. M. Haller, who, in turn, alerted the coroner's office and county detectives.

At 9:40 A.M., officers James Davison, Jack Lees, and Samuel J. Riddle arrived at the reclamation plant. Two deputy coroners, Donald Conners and Fred Wehagen, had arrived before them and had already removed the torso and the disarticulated limbs from the car's interior. Foul-smelling and discolored, the body was crawling with maggots and was so decomposed that the assembled lawmen couldn't even determine whether the torso belonged to a man or a woman. As a photographer took pictures of the car's interior and exterior, the detectives examined the spot where the body had been found. "There was no evidence of any kind to be found inside this car," wrote Officer Riddle in his formal report later that day, "and the body was nude and we were not able to find any clothing." After checking the history of the freight cars' movements over the past few months at the yardmaster's office, the trio of detectives returned to the reclamation plant at 11:15 A.M., only to be met by an unnerved Superintendent Haller. Harry Gross and fellow railroad worker John Kikel had stumbled on a second body in another freight car further down the same track. Even to hardened lawmen who had

THE DARKEST CIRCLES OF HELL

Yard of the P&LE Railroad in Stowe Township, Pennsylvania, where the three boxcar victims were discovered on May 3, 1940. Photograph by Paul Johnson.

seen it all, the scene inside car 51224 was deeply disquieting. A human corpse, decapitated and dismembered in the same manner as the first and as badly decomposed, lay in the darkness of the car's east end. "The legs and one arm were placed on the floor first and then the torso was placed neatly on top of them with the shoulders pointed toward the door," wrote Riddle in his report. Again, the official photographer snapped pictures of the disgusting scene; again, the officers endured the dank, fetid air of the car's interior as they combed the area for evidence. As at the earlier discovery, they found no clothing; but this time their search did yield forty paper bags bearing the label "Evert Fuel Co.," a circular piece of upholstery material, and a piece of checkered cloth five inches wide and thirty inches long. Just what all this debris added up to was anybody's guess.

Allegheny County's coroner, P. J. Henney, arrived at the plant with an assistant to take the second body to the morgue. (Riddle's report does not specify when the first body had been removed from the scene, but the official autopsy protocol indicates that the procedure was performed at 10:20 A.M. Conners and Wehagen must have taken the remains to the morgue almost immediately after the police had viewed the body.) However, since official word of the terrible discoveries had spread quickly, the district attorney, Andrew T. Park, accompanied by two more county detectives, also appeared on the scene. It was now 12:05 P.M., and as Henney and his assistants prepared to remove the body, a pale, shaken Harry Gross approached and informed the group that he and John Kikel had found yet a third body in another freight car. This latest news seemed stranger than the most outlandish piece of pulp fiction. Three bodies, all decapitated and mutilated, found close together but in separate boxcars within a single day? Surely this wasn't possible! The men walked silently down the line of freight cars as Gross led them to car 33850. What they witnessed then was the most mystifying and terrible crime scene yet in a day already filled with mind-numbing horrors. There seemed to be blood everywhere—pooled on the floor of the car and smeared on one of the walls. At the east end of the car, partly covered with sheathing paper, the men saw the nude, headless, badly decomposed body of a man lying on its back, the word *Nazi*—the z inverted—cut deeply into the flesh of the chest. Unlike the two victims found earlier, this man had obviously been killed and decapitated where he lay, and his limbs were still attached. Before investigators moved in for a closer inspection, the busy photographer documented the appalling spectacle. Police found several bits of evidence scattered about the floor: a piece of clothesline five inches long, two pearl buttons, a bone button, and two pieces of shoestring. Someone had obviously burned something; ashes and bits of scorched paper lay on the floor of the car. There were enough large, intact pieces left to determine that the paper had been the December 11, 1939, issue of the *Youngstown Vindicator*. Someone had stepped in the blood when it had been fresh and left behind a large, bloody footprint on one of the pieces of newspaper.

It was now early afternoon, but the shocking day was still not over. As Coroner Henney and his assistants transported the most recently discovered torso to the Allegheny County Morgue to be autopsied, police removed the blood-smeared side panels from the car as evidence. Official word of the terrible discoveries went out to the police departments of Cleveland, Youngtown, and New Castle. At 5:00 P.M.,

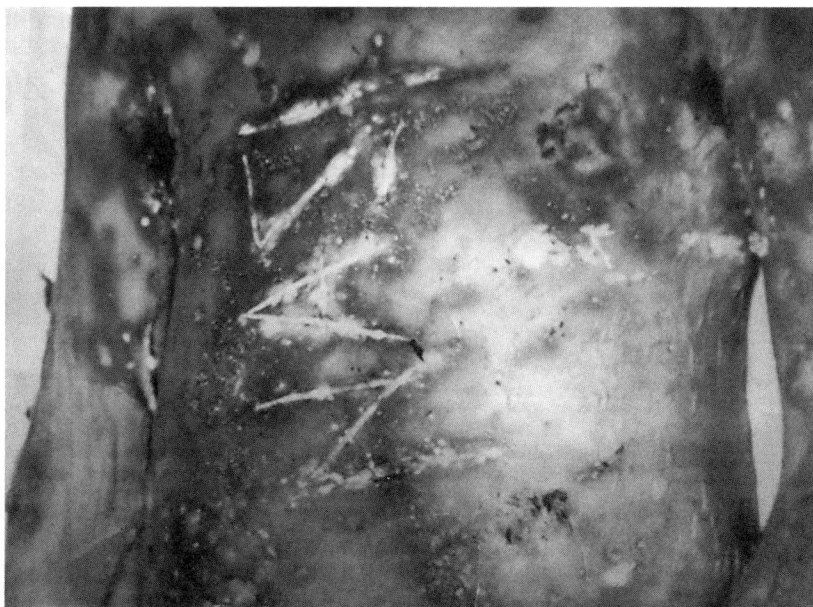

Corpse of James David Nicholson, shown in the only known surviving photograph of any of the boxcar victims. Photograph courtesy of the *Cleveland Plain Dealer*.

Youngstown's chief of police, John Turnbull, and chief of detectives William Reed arrived at the crime scene, followed shortly thereafter by men from Lawrence County and a contingent from Cleveland, notably Eliot Ness's assistant, Robert Chamberlin; David Cowles of the SIB; and, of course, Detective Merylo. (Although Riddle does not mention them in his report, subsequent newspaper stories, Merylo's own police reports, and his memoirs agree that Lloyd Trunk, Cowles's assistant, and Martin Zalewski, Merylo's partner, were also among the group that made the trip from Cleveland.) After visiting the morgue to view the remains and hear the preliminary results of the autopsies performed by the coroner's physician, Theodore R. Helmbold, all the assembled lawmen—now joined by Chief Robert Toussaint and Captain Cashmore of the P&LE Railroad Police, as well as officials from New Castle and Butler, Pennsylvania—met in the office of DA Park for a conference. It had been an extraordinary and very trying day; what had begun as a simple freight car inspection ended with a high-level meeting involving railroad police and ranking law enforcement officials from three different cities in two neighboring states. The most massive police investigation in Cleveland history had now spread far beyond the borders of Cuyahoga County. In his detailed report, submitted at the end of the day, Officer Samuel J. Riddle summed up the initial reactions of the men from Cleveland: "All were of the opinion that they had been killed by the same person who killed a number of other humans in a like manner in and around Cleveland and they refered [*sic*] to him as the 'Torso Murderer.'"

—

One by one, the three sets of human remains had reached the Allegheny County Morgue, and pathologist Theodore Helmbold had performed each autopsy immediately upon arrival: the victim designated as no. 1 at 10:20 A.M., to be followed by victim 2 at 1:45 P.M. and victim 3 at 2:50 P.M. Thus the preliminary results were already available when the contingent of officials arrived from Cleveland sometime after 5:00 P.M. Helmbold judged all three victims to be shorter than average and a bit heavy—no taller than five feet eight inches, and weighing about 160 pounds. His official protocols were concerned primarily with the condition of the bodies, the points of disarticulation, and the appearance of the internal organs; aside from a comment that the body of victim 1 may have been frozen at some point, he refrained from speculating as to cause of death and indulged in very little theorizing of any sort. Obviously, Helmbold's goal was to describe in minute detail what could clearly be discerned through visual observation. Although he surmised that all three had been killed anywhere from three weeks to several months before discovery, he didn't try to establish the amount of time that had elapsed between each murder and the next. The wording for his conclusions in all three cases was virtually identical. For victim 1 he wrote, "The examination of this body revealed no cause of death. The blood vessels of the body contained no blood and death could have resulted from hemorrhage. The cause of death may be in the head however, which was absent." The only difference for the second and third cases was his insertion of a single word before "body"—*dismembered* for victim 2 and *decapitated* for victim 3. Assuming the press was reporting his words accurately, however, Helmbold's public statements were considerably more specific. On May 4, the *Pittsburgh Post-Gazette* reported him as declaring that all three men were killed by the same person using the same weapon. One day earlier, on May 3, three new-papers revealed Helmbold's conclusion that the killer showed skill in cutting up the bodies. The *Pittsburgh Sun Telegraph* described the bodies as "neatly dismembered," adding, "The arm and leg joints were neatly and cleanly dissected, as though performed by a butcher or some person familiar with slaughter house work." The *Cleveland News* proclaimed that "they were dismembered by someone with a knowledge of surgery, medical officers said," adding the next day that the killer displayed "unusual skill in surgery." The *New Castle News* likewise noted that "all three corpses had been dismembered with medical precision." Despite the dreadful condition of all three bodies, the coroner's of-fice asked Pittsburgh's identification officer, Leo Dumont, if he could lift any useable fingerprints from the remains. He had arrived at the discovery scene at around 10:00 A.M. on May 3, remaining there until all the bodies had been sent off to the morgue. Employing the most cutting-edge forensic techniques then available, Dumont managed to get prints from two of the bodies; the fingers of the remaining victim had been burned to frustrate any attempt at identification. To get the prints, he severed the fingers from the limbs of the two corpses, sub-merged them in various chemical solutions for as long as seventy-two hours to bring out the ridge details, stuffed them with cotton to firm the rotting skin, and then carefully took prints, photographs of which were immediately dispatched to the FBI offices in Washington, D.C., for possible identification. The word *Nazi* carved into the chest of the third victim to be found remained the most perplexing and mysterious detail of the entire series of gruesome discoveries. Since the edges of the letters seemed jagged rather than smooth, and given the amount of deterioration, Helmbold couldn't say if the word had been carved with a knife or burned into the skin with acid. The crudity of the lettering and the backward *z* convinced some lawmen that the perpetrator was not well educated. Others wondered if the mutilation on the chest pointed to someone with strong anti-Nazi sentiments. But even that conjecture was questionable; the war in Europe had been raging for only eight months, and the United States was not yet involved.

The likelihood of a link between these newly discovered murders and the Cleveland killings remained a matter of debate among the assembled officials. While the *Cleveland Press* reported, on May 3, that "the skill with which they were dismembered gave rise to the speculation that

Cleveland's 'mad butcher of Kingsbury Run' may be at work again," Youngstown's police chief, John W. Turnbull, told the *Youngstown Vindicator* the next day, May 4, that he was convinced the crimes were local and had nothing to do with the murders in Cleveland. SIB head David Cowles was initially inclined to see a link, but remained characteristically cautious in his statements to the press. "We have much more material to work with than has been found in any of the other torso killings," he told the *Cleveland Press* on May 4, "though we still have no real clew [*sic*] to the killer's identity." The *Cleveland Plain Dealer* reported him the same day as acknowledging the similarity of method in decapitation and dismemberment, but also noted his warning that the decomposition of all three bodies recovered from the boxcars made such apparent similarities difficult to confirm. Detective Merylo, in contrast, was not hampered by any such troublesome doubts, nor was he the least bit shy about sharing his opinions with the gentlemen of the press, who eagerly reported whatever he had to say. Merylo had been convinced of a link between the murders in Cleveland and those in New Castle since 1937, and he had no qualms about adding these three new victims to the Butcher's tally. "It must have been the same killer in all these cases," he assured the *Cleveland Press* on May 4. "All were beheaded in the same way. A medical examination shows the same skill in dissection"—a judgment he readily shared with the *Pittsburgh Post-Gazette* the same day. He told the *Pittsburgh Sun Telegraph,* also on May 4, that he thought the killer must be a big man who was following the newspaper accounts of his crimes and using different methods to obscure the identity of his victims to confuse police. In succeeding decades, when the histories of the torso murders came to be written, it was Peter Merylo's certainty that commentators would remember, rather than the equivocations and doubts of his colleagues.

—

By May 1940, the war in Europe was entering its ninth month, but for at least three days, the rumble of Nazi tanks took second place in the local press of northeastern Ohio and western Pennsylvania to the horrors found in the freight cars of Stowe Township. Newspapers in Cleveland, Youngstown, Pittsburgh, and New Castle covered the discovery of the grisly "cargo of death" and reported in great detail any new developments in the investigation over the next few days—easily the most extensive coverage any of the killings attributed to the Mad Butcher had ever received. Initial police uncertainty about the gender of the first body Gross found was repeated and enlarged upon in the first newspaper stories to appear; both the first and second victims were incorrectly identified as female. At the meeting in DA Park's office at the end of the day on May 3, the assembled officials decided to return to the discovery sites the next morning to look for additional evidence that might have been missed. The odyssey of the dilapidated freight cars before their arrival in Stowe Township was double-checked, and police reports were revisited in a search for any stray details or clues related to the discoveries whose significance may have been initially overlooked. In Youngstown, railroad workers systematically checked nearly two hundred freight cars destined for dismantling at the Stowe Township reclamation plant. Some railroad workers recalled finding a bundle of blood-soaked clothing, in late December 1939, in a freight car belonging to the same string where the bodies were ultimately found. Two shirts, a couple of men's suits, a pair of work shoes, some underwear, and a denim jacket had been wrapped in an overcoat and tied with a belt. When police had duly looked into the matter, they had learned nothing beyond the fact that the overcoat bore the label of a clothing store in Cincinnati. The bundle ultimately disappeared when police moved to new headquarters. In late February 1940, while the string of dilapidated cars had been sitting in Struthers, Ohio, there had been a mysterious fire in one of the cars, suspiciously close to the three later found to contain human remains. Authorities now sifted through what remained of the ashes, operating on the belief that the killer might have set the fire in an attempt to burn the heads or, possibly, even another body.

The two-state investigation immediately swung into high gear. Authorities quickly established the full history of the derelict cars' movements in the months before the corpses were found. The cars had stood neglected on a P&LE Railroad side track in Youngstown from December 1938 until April 19, 1940, when workers moved the string to Struthers, Ohio. Two days later, they were moved again to McKees Rocks, near Pittsburgh, and finally, on May 2, to the reclamation plant in Stowe Township. Given the condition of the corpses, this history suggested that all three victims had been killed in Youngstown. Police from Cleveland, Pittsburgh, Youngstown, and New Castle rode the rails

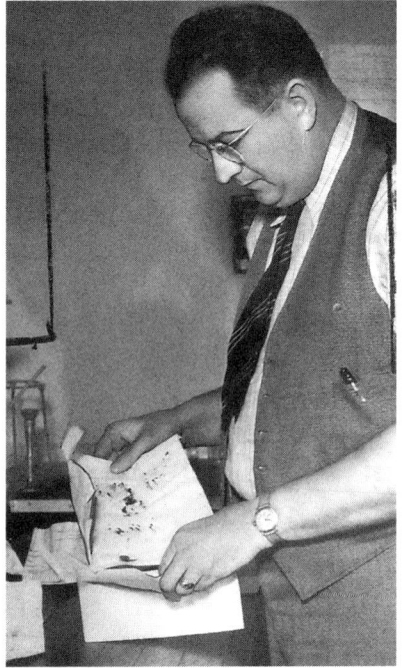

David Cowles, the head of Cleveland's Criminal Identification Bureau and one of Eliot Ness's most trusted associates, left, and his assistant, Lloyd Trunk. The two men were among the contingent of law enforcement personnel who visited Pennsylvania periodically between 1938 and 1940. Photographs courtesy of the *Cleveland Plain Dealer*.

to retrace the odyssey—the "death route," as the newspapers termed it—of the nineteen derelict cars, stopping in both Youngstown and Struthers, in a largely fruitless search for additional clues in the rail yards of the P&LE Railroad. A few possible clues did come to light, though. In Stowe Township, they recovered seventy-some strands of human hair of two different colors, additional bits of paper bearing bloody heel marks, and the butt of a marijuana cigarette. A check of missing person reports in Youngstown and Struthers yielded nothing. Since only two of the twelve recognized victims of the Cleveland torso murders had been positively identified, the police there had operated on the assumption that the killer was picking his targets from among the castoffs of society who gathered in the shanty towns of the Flats and Kingsbury Run. Thinking along similar lines, Youngstown police were especially interested in a hobo jungle called Hoover City, a thirty-six-year-old huddle of dilapidated shacks fairly close to the spot where the boxcars had been sitting while in Struthers. Acting on the very real possibility that the three still-unidentified bodies might be former residents of Hoover City, police moved in and interviewed the inhabitants. This was not an easy task; the population was transient and identity could be difficult to establish among the down and out. The municipal incinerator for the city of Youngstown stood adjacent to Hoover City, prompting the authorities to wonder if the three missing heads might have been burned there.

Within the next couple of days, police caught a major break. Dumont's careful attempt to lift useable prints from the hands of two of the corpses paid off. The Ohio State Bureau of Criminal Identification in London, Ohio, reported that the fingerprints of the third victim belonged to a thirty-year-old ex-convict named James David Nicholson, alias James Henderson, whose last known address was in Chicago. For the first time in the history of the butcheries found in New Castle's Murder Swamp and along the Pennsylvania railroad, police had an identity with which to work: Nicholson had a personal history that could be uncovered, movements that could be traced, family and friends that could be tracked down and interviewed. And Nicholson had a very colorful history. He had begun his criminal career with a 1928 burglary charge in Kenosha, Wisconsin, when he was eighteen. He went on to a life of arrests and incarcerations in Illinois, Michigan, Wisconsin, Virginia, and South Carolina for larceny, burglary, trespass, turning in false alarms, and parole violations. Unfortunately, all evidence of Nicholson's sordid career ended in late 1939—two to six months before his horrible death—when he seems to have fallen off the grid and descended into the grueling life of a transient, aimlessly riding the rails from one location to the next. As a down-and-outer moving through a twilight world on the fringes of society, Nicholson perfectly fit the profile of the Cleveland Butcher's victims. What paths he may have taken in the last months of his life, before he wound up naked, beheaded, and mutilated in a boxcar in Stowe Township, remain a total mystery. Since authorities never learned anything about Nicholson's political beliefs or affiliations, the word *Nazi* carved on his chest was never explained.

Meanwhile, a second discovery threatened to seriously complicate, if not actually derail, the investigation. Microscopic examination of the

James David Nicholson, the only one of the three boxcar victims discovered on May 3, 1940, to be positively identified. Drawing by Michael Nevin from a lost newspaper photograph.

vertebrae of the neck in one of the victims—unfortunately, it is not clear from the press coverage which of the three was being referred to—revealed the marks of a small-toothed saw (most likely a Gigli saw) rather than a knife. If true, this discovery had the potential to undermine the theory that these boxcar murders were related to the Cleveland killings and shift the whole nature of the investigation. The Cleveland Butcher had never used a saw. A Gigli saw is an old and rather simple medical instrument, often used in brain surgery for cutting through bone. Somewhat resembling a child's jump rope, its design consists of a wire and thin blade attached to two handles. The surgeon saws through the bone simply by pulling the handles back and forth. I've seen film of the Gigli saw being used to cut through a patient's skull. Not only did the head have to be stabilized in some manner but the surgeon's hands, while pulling the device back and forth, tended to work at a level

BUREAU OF POLICE
DIVISION OF CRIMINAL IDENTIFICATION
PITTSBURGH, PA.

The following is the record of Pittsburgh --- No. Decapitated Murder Victim # 3.

NAME AND NUMBER	ARRESTED OR RECEIVED AND DATE	CHARGE AND DISPOSITION
James David Nickelson # B-337	Arr. PD Waukegan Ill March 13, 1929	Burglary, turned over to PD at Libertyville Illinois.
James D. Nicholson # A-9531	Recd. St.Reformatory Pontiac Ill.11-29-29	Larceny, 1 to 10 years.Paroled on 3-25-33; Returned as parole violtr 5-17-33; Re-Paroled 10-3-34
Leslie Nicholson 26878	Arr. PD Milwaukee Wisc. 10-9-34	Turning in False Alarms & Parole violator.Turned over to Parole Agent, Chicago Ill.
James D. Nichols 13024	Recd. St.Penty @ Menard Ill 6-13-35 in transfer from St.Penty @ Pontiac Ill.	Larceny, 1 to 10 years.
James David Nicholson 26878	Arr. PD Milwaukee Wis 4-29-36	Burglary.
James David Nicholson 22951	Recd. State Prison @ Waupun Wis;5-4-36	Burglary; 1 to 3 years.Released on Parole 4-20-38;Final Disch.11-4-38
James David Nicholson 2088	Arr.PD Petersburg Va. 5-8-39	Pulling False Alarm, Fined $100.00 and costs.
James David Nicholson #	Arr. PD, Richmond Va. June 6, 1939	Lodger, released.
James Nicholson 7850 " " 8121 " " 8174	PD Greenville S.C; 7-28-1939;Tresp Southern RR,$15-30 days. PD Greenville S.C;10-28-1939; Transient, No disposition. PD Greenville S.C;11-4- 1939; Transient, No disposition.	
Subject admits 1928	Kenosha Wisc; Burglary;	1 year Probation.
Victim # 3.	Police Department, PITTSBURGH PA.	Inquiry May 10, 1940.
FBI # 839169		

James David Nicholson's rap sheet. This record of his criminal history is included in the coroner's files from Allegheny County, Pennsylvania. Photograph courtesy of the University of Pittsburgh. Allegheny County, Pa., Coroner's Office Records, 1884–1976. AIS.1982.07, Archives Service Center, University of Pittsburgh.

somewhat below the operating table. These limitations would make such a saw extremely difficult to use on a broad, flat surface, like the floor of a boxcar; although it just might be possible to loop the blade under the victim's neck and pull upward, such a technique would be awkward and difficult. David Cowles collected some of the vertebrae from the Allegany County Coroner's Office for further examination back in Cleveland. Interestingly, the work was to be performed, not at the Cuyahoga County Morgue by local pathologists, but by anatomists at the Western Reserve University Medical School—the first signs that someone high up in Cleveland's echelons of authority had decided to bypass Dr. Samuel Gerber and the local coroner's office. There is no surviving evidence as to whether the examination in Cleveland substantiated the findings from Pittsburgh or not. The press did not print any follow-up articles, and if any paper work was completed at Western Reserve's medical school, it was either destroyed or simply lost in the archival clutter.

—

Two fascinating documents are filed with the autopsy protocols of these three victims. It would be rather easy to overlook them among the assembled affidavits, depositions, and formal papers from the coroner's office and even easier to miss their stunning significance. The first is a telegram dated May 15, 1940, from Cleveland's police chief, George Matowitz, to the coroner of Alleghany County, P. J. Henney. It reads, "Request permission to transport bodies of torsos to Cleveland at our expense for examination by our pathologist at medical school rather than immediate cremation." A day or so later, a professional undertaker from Cleveland arrived in Pittsburgh bearing the second document: a letter of introduction from Matowitz, dated May 17: "This letter will serve to introduce to you [Coroner Henney] Mr. David I. Jones, duly licensed undertaker of this city, who is in your city for the purpose of returning the three Torso's [sic] found in your county." The letter goes on to say that the remains will be turned over to Dr. Normand Hoerr at the Western Reserve University Medical School. The only individual copied on the letter was David Cowles, head of the Scientific Identification Bureau in Cleveland. The implications of all this maneuvering are startlingly clear; the coroner of Cuyahoga County was being deliberately bypassed. The chief of police and the head of the SIB—no doubt with the approval of, or perhaps even at the behest of, Safety Director Ness—were actively keeping the duly elected coroner of Cuyahoga County, Samuel R. Gerber, out of the loop!

In 1940, Gerber was into the fourth year of his half-century tenure as county coroner. He had been elected in 1936, replacing Arthur J. Pearce, who had been on the job during the twelve-month period (September 1935 to September 1936) when the first six of the Butcher's officially recognized twelve victims were discovered. It would be easy to dismiss this bit of chicanery as petty politics—to assume that the safety director, the chief of police, and the mayor, all Republicans, were simply trying to snub the coroner, a Democrat. But the evidence is quite clear: creeping dissatisfaction, even distrust, of the Cuyahoga County Coroner's Office had been developing for at least three years.

The first sign of this unfortunate state of affairs surfaced in the summer of 1937, when Peter Merylo brought in a pathologist from City Hospital, apparently with Gerber's consent, to examine the pieces of victim 9. No explanation for this move was given, but it would seem that someone in authority was entertaining questions, if not doubts, about someone or something in the coroner's office. A year later, one of Ness's assistants, Robert Chamberlin, precipitated a major brouhaha in the press when he announced publicly that the safety director's office wanted an outside expert to examine a part of victim 10 to "corroborate his [the coroner's] findings." Gerber reacted to this obvious questioning of his office's competence with predictable indignation; no outside expert would be allowed to encroach on his territory. Then came the disastrous bungling of the examination of victim 11 by Gerber's office in August 1938. The autopsy had been performed by county pathologist Reuben Straus. He declared that the corpse, that of a woman, had probably been a murder victim, but he added that he couldn't be sure of the cause, and Gerber had blithely signed off on Straus's findings. The pieces of the victim were ultimately turned over to the anatomy department of the Western Reserve University Medical School, where they were duly examined by Dr. T. Windgate Todd. Suddenly, Todd summoned David Cowles to his office. In total disgust, the anatomist showed Cowles the body parts that had been sent over from the morgue. The coroner's office had made a major blunder: the body parts they had sent Todd were not the remains of a legitimate torso victim but

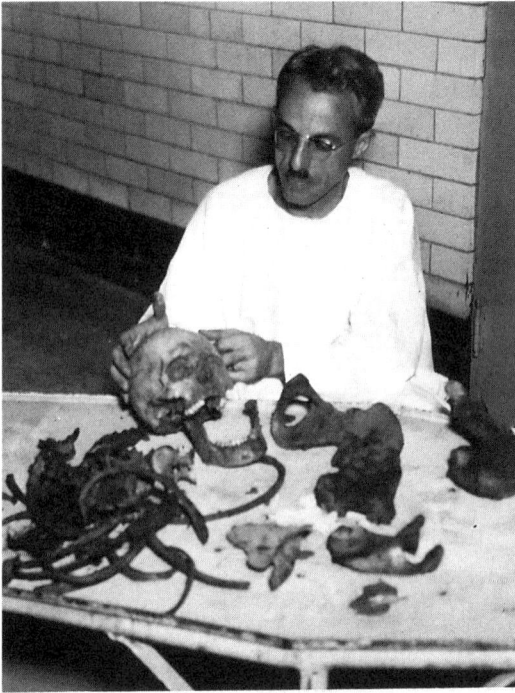

Samuel Gerber, the coroner of Ohio's Cuyahoga County, shown here with the skeletal remains of Cleveland victim 12. The Cleveland Police Department and the safety director's office kept Gerber out of the loop during the investigation of the Pennsylvania killings. Photograph from the *Cleveland Press* archives; courtesy of Cleveland State University.

pieces of a body that had already been embalmed! A mistake of this magnitude in such a high-profile case was simply unacceptable, and the sloppiness it exhibited raised troubling questions about the other autopsies over which Gerber had presided. Moreover, since Cowles knew about this blunder, there can be no doubt that Eliot Ness, and perhaps even Chief Matowitz, did as well.

The decision in 1940 to pass over Gerber had no legal implications; the coroner of Cuyahoga County would have no jurisdiction over bodies found in another county in another state. If Gerber knew anything about this very deliberate slap in the face, he held his silence. This potentially explosive secret did not escape the relatively narrow circle of Ness confidants until David Cowles broke his silence during a 1983 interview, and by then, the Kingsbury Run murders were very old news; no one took any notice of his stunning revelation.

The question of whether these three Stowe Township victims had been dispatched, decapitated, and otherwise mutilated by Cleveland's Mad Butcher was vitally important to the conduct of the investigation, too important to allow for any sloppiness or mistakes. Hence a pathologist at Western Reserve University's Medical School was asked to handle the official examination. Normand Hoerr had been on the staff for about a year in 1940. Just how he wound up with this crucially important assignment is unclear. He may have been recommended by Todd, or, perhaps, Ness and Cowles wanted someone new to do the job—someone with fresh eyes who was relatively unprejudiced by the past history of Kingsbury Run. Unfortunately, there is no extant record of Hoerr's findings. Had the bodies been turned over to the coroner's office in Cuyahoga County, a paper trail of some sort would have survived; however, the three Stowe Township victims and further findings about them simply vanished when David I. Jones drove up to the Western Reserve University Medical School and delivered his ghastly cargo to Normand Hoerr.

NOTES

Most of the information concerning the body discovered in October 1939 and the subsequent investigation comes from the *New Castle News,* the *Cleveland Press,* and the *Cleveland News.* Other significant details have been culled from Detective Peter Merylo's official police report of October 21, 1939.

The three corpses discovered in Stowe Township boxcars on May 3, 1940, received the most extensive coverage of any chapter in the history of the torso murders. The *Cleveland Press,* the *Cleveland News,* the *Cleveland Plain Dealer,* the *Youngstown Vindicator,* the *New Castle News,* the *Pittsburgh Post-Gazette,* the *Pittsburgh Sun Telegraph,* and the *Pittsburgh Press* ran front-page, headline stories of the discovery and its aftermath for three days. Additional information comes from the three autopsy protocols written by the Allegheny County pathologist, officially designated as C-40-34, C-40-35, and C-40-36. The county files also contain signed affidavits from those involved, police reports from those on the scene, and correspondence with officials in other municipalities. Other details come from Peter Merylo's official police reports and his memoirs. When any discrepancies or inconsistencies arose between Merylo's reports and his memoirs, I invariably relied on the former, those documents being much closer in time to the events being recorded.

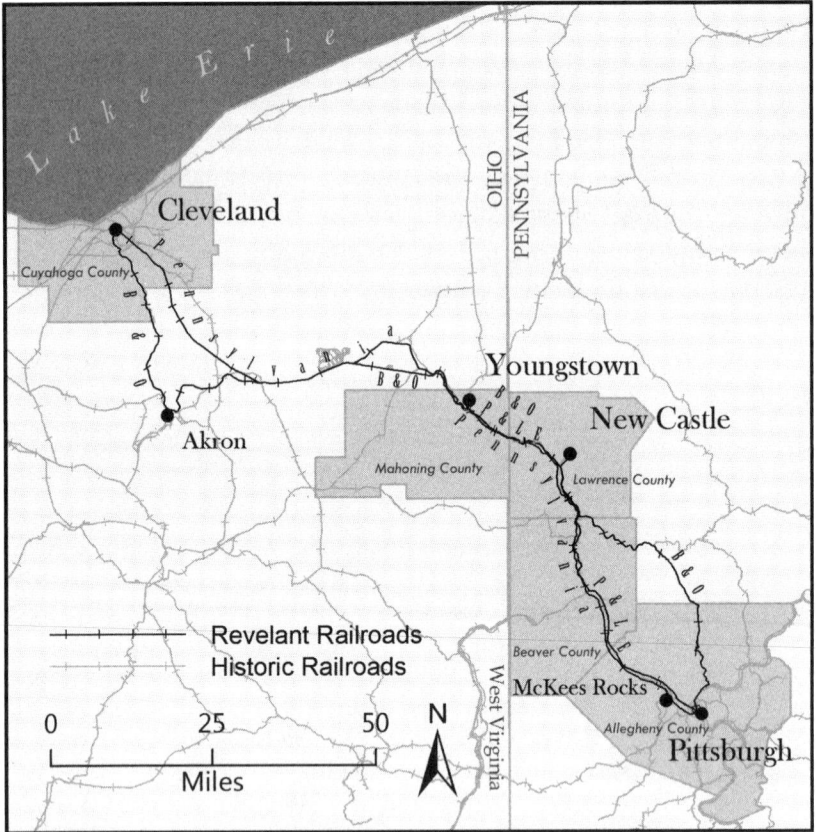

The railroad lines linking Cleveland, Youngstown, Pittsburgh, and New Castle. Map by Luke Moussa.

CHAPTER 5

ODYSSEY INTO THE ABYSS

The stark realities of the Great Depression may have largely faded from American public memory, but the graphic images from that era of transients riding the railroad lines through the lonely desolation and decay of large industrial cities remain vivid. The gloomy menace of boxcars and gondolas on lonely sidings silhouetted against the night sky; the hollow, distant shriek of the steam engine's whistle and the haunting clack of car wheels running over miles of iron track; the fleeting glimpses of raggedly dressed men scrambling to hop aboard a slow-moving freight train; the utter poverty of the hobo jungles and shanty towns that grew and festered close to the rail lines—such lingering images and echoes of America's desperation at that time retain their depressing power. Ever since early September 1936, when he was assigned full-time to the torso murders by George Matowitz, Cleveland's chief of police, Detective Peter Merylo thought that this ugly nightmare world of transients somehow held the key to solving the sickening series of decapitation murders that had been terrifying Clevelanders for at least two years. He made his first foray into the abyss almost immediately after receiving his marching orders from Matowitz. "I've rarely been afraid," Merylo insists in his memoirs, "but I'll confess to hair-raising, spine-chilling fear one night late in September, 1936, when I put on the oldest clothes I had, let my beard grow and stalked the killer through the Run." He spent most of that time prowling through a dark tunnel that led to a railway "repair shop"—though he does not specify whether the shop belonged to the railroads or to the Cleveland transit line—or in the dingy, junk-filled shop itself. This brief taste of the darkness and gloom of society's underbelly would be only a preliminary warm-up for the odyssey to come.

The triple horror of Stowe Township on May 3, 1940, left Merylo more convinced than ever that the railroads held the key to solving the mystery of the torso murders. Chief Matowitz had always been a little reluctant to let his ace detective face the very real dangers of the hobo world and lifestyle by going underground, so it must have come as something of a surprise when the chief approached Merylo in early July 1940 to ask the detective if he was still interested in pursuing the elusive killer by going undercover and riding the rails that linked Cleveland, Youngstown, New Castle, and Pittsburgh. Matowitz's reasons for making this request are not on record. The three bodies found in Stowe Township had been discovered only two months earlier, so Matowitz may have been responding either to the results of David Cowles's tests on the recovered neck vertebrae of one of the victims or to Normand Hoerr's examination of all three corpses at the Western Reserve Medical School. Perhaps, just perhaps, Cowles or Hoerr found something that pointed to a possible link between the murder victims of Cleveland and those of western Pennsylvania. Whatever Matowitz's reasoning, Merylo did not wait to be asked twice.

Going "on the bum," however, would not be easy. If there was any information to be gathered among the transients, Merylo would have to blend in; he would have to look and act like those dwelling on society's margins to gain their trust. He would have to travel with them, eat with them, and occasionally bunk down with them. To complicate matters further, there was no possibility that Merylo could undertake an assignment this dangerous alone, and finding a willing partner would be difficult. Merylo and his long-time partner, Martin Zalewski, had clashed over a minor investigative procedure, and relations between the two men had cooled. Furthermore, Zalewski was nearing the end of his twenty-five-year stint on the Cleveland police force, and he was reluctant to end his tenure with such a grueling and dangerous assignment. When Merylo approached other colleagues in the department, their initial interest in joining him undercover subsided when they learned that they were really going to have to live like bums and mix with a lot of "perverts and screwballs." Finally, though, Merylo found a willing partner. "I was down in front of City Hall one morning," Merylo wrote in his memoirs, "and ran into Frank Vorell who was sitting in an

Accident Prevention Squad car. He was in uniform and I just thought I'd ask, knowing he was related by marriage to Frank Dolezal and probably had a more than average interest in seeing this torso mystery

Peter Merylo poses for the camera before going "on the bum." The dedication in the upper right corner reads, "To my good friend Honorable Judge Samuel H. Silbert from other Merylo while on Torso Murder Hunt in 1940." Photograph courtesy of the Merylo family and the Cleveland Police Historical Society.

cleared up." (Frank Dolezal had been arrested and falsely accused in the torso killings and eventually wound up dead in his jail cell—an alleged suicide—before the city's legal machinery could deal with him fully. See the notes at the end of this chapter for a fuller explanation of Frank Dolezal's supposed link with the case.) Whatever reasons he may have had, personal or otherwise, Vorell readily agreed to join Merylo in the twilight world of social outcasts. Procedural *i*'s had to be dotted and *t*'s crossed, however, so on July 12, 1940, Merylo formally asked his immediate superior, Lieutenant Harvey Weitzel, for official "permission to go out of town on police business." "I request that I be permitted to go to Youngtown, Ohio and New Castle, Pa. where I will devote my entire time in the HOBO camps and other jungles in that vicinity and also ride freight trains between Kingsbury Run this city and New Castle, Pa. with a view of apprehending the person or persons responsible for our torso murders."

On Saturday, July 13, 1940, Peter Merylo began his odyssey into society's dark and ominous nether world. Now sporting a few days' growth of beard and in need of a haircut, he gathered together some scruffy clothing and drove by himself to Youngstown, ahead of Frank Vorell, armed with little more than his finely honed instincts as a cop and his now unshakable conviction that the hobo jungles and railways of northeastern Ohio and western Pennsylvania held the elusive key to the murder-dismemberments in both states. Once in Youngstown, Merylo checked in with that city's chief of police, John Turnbull, alerting him to his plans and asking that his presence in the area be kept secret. (It is interesting to note at this point that Matowitz apparently had not given his counterpart in Youngstown an official notice of Merylo's assignment.) Then he searched for a suitably dingy, out-of-the-way rooming house—a base of operations to which he could retreat and decompress. "I wanted something in keeping with my new role of hobo, transient, itinerant and indigent visitor in Youngstown," he wrote in his memoirs. "A neighborhood from which I wouldn't be missed and in which I wouldn't attract attention. A place where my comings and goings wouldn't be questioned too closely. No gossipy landladies; no inquisitive neighbors." He eventually found what he was looking for on Poland Avenue, relatively close to the railroad siding where the three headless bodies had been discovered two months earlier—a joint so dilapidated and poor that the only shower was a made-over coal bin in the filthy basement. Apparently no one else living there cared much for bodily hygiene; the shower head was so crusted over with rust that Merylo had to free up some of the holes with a toothpick. But the flop house was exactly what he was looking for; and at a mere $3.00 per week, it was a bargain.

This underground odyssey remains the most minutely and precisely detailed operation in the entire history of the torso murders investigation. Merylo not only wrote extensively about his and Vorell's adventures undercover in both of his memoirs but he also covered it minutely in his sixteen-page, single-spaced report to his superiors, a report which survives intact in his collection of official papers. On July 14, his first day in the field, Merylo learned how deeply the lives of local transients had been affected by the torso murder investigation. When he went prowling around the city incinerator looking for the hobo encampment that had been close by for years, he discovered the place deserted. Later in the

A candid shot of Frank Vorell (standing) with an unidentified transient, taken during his and Merylo's weeks underground. Photograph courtesy of the Merylo family and Mary Dolezal Satterlee.

day, he managed to find about a dozen men living in a makeshift camp close to the Mahoning River. They told him that police had raided the incinerator camp earlier and carted the residents off to jail. The few men Merylo found had managed to escape the dragnet, which one of the men insisted had been a response to the torso murders. After checking a number of boxcars for any sign of tampering, Merylo hung around the post office, waiting for his new partner to arrive from Cleveland. Vorell drove to Youngstown with his wife and sons, and after kissing them goodbye, he joined Merylo in the gloomy dwelling the two men would call home until Matowitz terminated the assignment in August.

The next day, Merylo and Vorell had their first dangerous lesson in living as vagrants. Hopping a freight heading for New Castle, they hung on for dear life to the rail of a tank car's catwalk as the train thundered over twenty miles of uneven tracks at a teeth-rattling seventy miles per hour. Apparently, riding a freight is like riding a horse; one has to learn how to hold on and absorb the shocks without bouncing. Frank Vorell picked up the skill more quickly than his partner, and Merylo had to study and imitate the younger man's body positions to keep from being thrown from the fast-moving train to a certain death. Once in the New Castle–West Pittsburg area, the two men fought their way into the fringes of the treacherous Murder Swamp in search of hobo camps, only to find them all deserted—perhaps because of the police or perhaps from fear of the torso murderer. After scouting around the railroad yards of West Pittsburg, the two weary men boarded a coal car, along with three transients, and headed back to home base in Youngstown. It had been an extraordinarily tiring and depressingly unproductive day.

The task facing Merylo and Vorell was staggeringly difficult—perhaps even impossible. First of all, they were newcomers in a world of outcasts, men who did not trust outsiders easily. Secondly, when questioning the tramps they could find, they had to stay in character, presenting themselves as a couple of down-and-out guys picking up stray bits of information about local affairs rather than cops interrogating witnesses. Thirdly, they were seriously handicapped by how little information they had. They first tried tracking the killer through his victims, but this tactic proved exceedingly difficult. Merylo carried a photograph of James Nicholson, the only western Pennsylvania victim to be positively identified, but it wasn't much use. What could he do with it? A tramp looking for an old buddy does not usually have a formal portrait of the man for whom he is searching. His only other concrete point of entry into casual questioning was the possible description of the victim of October 1939 culled from railroad workers, who recalled an effeminate blond man hanging around the yards; accordingly, Merylo asked about a missing old friend—a blond man with curly hair.

Next, remembering the marijuana cigarette butt investigators had recovered at the site of the Stowe Township killings, Merylo tried to track the killer through the illegal drug trade. Discreet inquires eventually led them to a seedy area around Watt and Front Streets in Youngstown, where they loitered among "a mixed population of Greeks, Italians, Mexicans, and colored." But the two men were new to the area, and the locals rebuffed their initial attempts to "score." Finally they were directed to a secretive local peddler, ultimately identified as James Ferraro—a man who had already served time for distributing drugs—who was willing to sell them a reefer and two matches for seventeen cents. After the sale, the mysterious supplier assured Merylo he could get as many cigarettes as they wanted. Over the next couple of days, the now-affable Ferraro supplied Merylo and Vorell with several reefers at various prices, including one transaction of ten for $1.00. Then he mysteriously disappeared, and many of the detectives' attempts to hook up with the elusive peddler came up empty. Finally, at around 6:10 P.M. on August 4, they tracked him down and arrested him on the corner of Boardman and Watt, turning him over to the Youngstown police for questioning. "James Ferraro may be the man who may be able to tell us of a good suspect in these crimes. He will be questioned in connection with same," Merylo wrote in his final report. At this late date it is impossible to say whether this slim hope, pinned on nothing more substantial than a marijuana cigarette butt found on the scene of the May 3, 1940, discoveries, ever led to anything even remotely useful to the faltering investigation. After his arrest, the mysterious Ferraro simply vanishes from the recorded history of the torso murders.

Merylo and Vorell repeatedly returned to the hobo jungles around the Youngstown municipal incinerator, the fringes of Murder Swamp, and areas near the railroad lines and sidings. The populations of the various camps were always in a state of flux, and even the locations of the hobo camps shifted constantly, largely because of police crackdowns. In their attempts to get friendly with camp residents, the two cops often had to join them for a meager, usually rather disgusting meal. In all their talks around the campfire, Merylo would casually turn the conversation to the infamous murders that had been occurring for years in the New Castle–West Pittsburg area. Did anyone remember them? Did anyone know anything about them? Had anyone ever heard a story about a possible suspect? Had there ever been any rumors of any kind? Time and again, the two cops were assured by the transients that the Murder Swamp killings were the result of bootleg wars in Youngstown and Pittsburgh, an opinion that Merylo obviously did not accept. A couple of times, the two men caught freight trains back to Cleveland to consult with Chief Matowitz and see their families, but returns to the comforts of home were brief: as evening neared, the duo usually hopped a freight back to their base in the shabby Youngstown rooming house. They also visited West Pittsburg to touch base with Constable Walter Bannon. He told them that things had been quiet in the swamp that year but added that he expected transient activity in the region to pick up in the fall. A new hobo camp had formed near a spring, but when Bannon's son Francis escorted the two Cleveland cops there, it was deserted.

Any sense of progress in the investigation ultimately proved ephemeral; whatever flimsy leads the two cops uncovered always petered out eventually. Their dedication and perseverance were admirable, but they were grasping at straws. Two incidents in particular demonstrate the paucity and the flimsiness of the leads Merylo and Vorell followed and the maddening futility they faced: the story of the Croatian suspect and the saga of Isabel Eddy's Bible. The first incident began with the detectives' initial encounter with the unnamed Croatian on July 17, when the two men were canvassing one of the remaining hobo jungles, trying to unearth any information at all on the three bodies discovered on May 3. Just why this particular transient attracted Merylo's attention is difficult to determine. Perhaps it was simply proximity: the Croatian admitted he had slept in the same string of derelict freight cars in which the three corpses were found, close to the time they were apparently killed. Whatever the reason, Merylo's gut told him the man probably knew more than he was saying. "We have no good reason to believe that he is the killer," Merylo concedes in his report. "However, if we are convinced that he has more information than he gave us, we will ask the Youngstown Police Dept. to take him into custody for further questioning." The next day, Merylo and Vorell approached the Croatian for a second time and asked him to go over his story again. Merylo later wrote in his report, "We showed him the photograph of [James] David Nicholson, one of the torso victims and informed him that the Youngstown Police gave us his photograph after we spent the night in jail. Telling us that there is a $1000.00 reward if we would learn the identity of the man that was with Nicholson at the time he was murdered. The Croatian looked at the photo of Nicholson and made some remark leading to religion which we could not understand."

That was enough for Merylo. On July 19, he phoned William Reed, Youngstown's chief of detectives, described the Croatian and his approximate location, and asked Reed to take the man into custody for questioning "as to how long he slept [*sic*] in the boxcars where the three headless bodies were found and who slept there with him." In order to protect their cover, Merylo felt it best that he and Frank Vorell not participate in the interview. In any event, though, Merylo's instincts proved fallible; the nameless Croatian had held nothing back, and no additional information came out of the interrogation.

The second incident began on July 30, when a Youngstown newspaper carried an intriguing story about a small Bible that investigators had recovered in an abandoned boxcar. Some verses from St. John had been underlined in red ink. The first, John 6:55, read, "For my flesh is meat indeed, and my blood is drink indeed"; a second, John 6:56, read, "He that eateth my flesh and drinketh my blood, dwelleth in me, and I in him." Considering that the Bible had been discovered during an investigation into some very grisly murders, those passages set off real alarm bells, prompting further investigation.

The Bible contained the name and address of the previous owner: Isabel Eddy, of 170 Garfield Avenue in Youngstown. When Merylo and Vorell canvassed the neighborhood and spoke to some of the residents familiar with the Bible's owner, they gradually put together a bizarre portrait of an apparent religious fanatic. Eddy's former landlord insisted that she belonged to a sect of holy rollers and constantly attended religious meetings either in a church building or a tent. Once when she returned from a service, he told the detectives, he heard her belt out a hardy, "I got the Lord" as she ascended the stairs. Mrs. Eddy had a husband, two young daughters in their early teens, and a misplaced heart of gold. One Christmas, she gave her minister $10.00 even though her own children had no shoes. On another occasion, she presented a neighbor with a bottle of grape juice, explaining that her religion taught her to share anything she had in abundance. Former neighbors of the Eddys told Merylo and Vorell that Youngstown police had already searched the area, trying to track her down. "From all indication and all preliminary investigation, this bible appears to be the best lead yet uncovered," an enthusiastic Merylo wrote in his final report.

The next day, Merylo learned from the Youngstown chief of police, Turnbull, that Detective Earl Hoffman had already found and interviewed Isabel Eddy in depth. She had given the Bible, Mrs. Eddy explained, to a "very nervous" tramp somewhere between the ages of thirty-five and forty-five who looked Irish, said little, and avoided eye contact. When Hoffman inquired about the passages marked in red ink, she insisted that she had marked the passages since she read them to her pupils in the Bible classes she taught. Before looking any further into Isabel Eddy and her affairs, Merylo felt that he and Vorell should see the Bible, which was then being held by Alleghany County detectives. Once they finally got it in their hands and began looking through it, their initial enthusiasm quickly faded. Several passages in addition to the two originally quoted in the newspaper had been marked with red ink or red pencil, and these others were nowhere near as luridly provocative as the two printed in the Youngstown paper. "Therefore, from all indications," a discouraged Merylo later wrote in his report, "these two verses quoted in the newspaper where [sic] singled out to make a good newspaper story." A more thorough search into Eddy's background revealed nothing more interesting than that she was a former loose woman of multiple affairs turned religious fanatic. A frustrated Peter Myerlo concluded that neither she nor her Bible had anything to do with the torso murders.

Rather like Kingsbury Run, its counterpart in Cleveland, the notorious Murder Swamp between New Castle and West Pittsburg seemed to grip Merylo's imagination. At times it was not even clear what he was looking for; he simply returned to the desolate area over and over again, perhaps to soak up the atmosphere, perhaps hoping to find something—anything—that had been previously overlooked. But tramping around the vast stretch of tangled vegetation and oozing muck was exceedingly dangerous for someone not familiar with the hidden trails and unaware of some of the potential hazards. The railroads had been using the swamp as a convenient dumping ground for hot ash and cinders for decades, and some of this discarded material would smolder for years, most likely mixing with the quicksand-like terrain to form a deadly mixture of hot ooze. On one occasion, Merylo nearly lost his life when he missed his footing and plunged into the hot mess up to his armpits. Desperately, he reached for a nearby loose railroad tie and managed to pull himself to safety.

The real dangers Merylo and Vorell faced during their time under-cover were counterbalanced by false alarms and frustrations, some of which bordered on high comedy. One evening, while walking along the railroad tracks, the two cops encountered a pair of suspicious-looking transients, each of whom carried something loosely wrapped with brown paper under their arms. From the dimensions of the mysterious packages, Merylo judged they could contain butcher knives. The two cops continued to stroll nonchalantly down the tracks, trying to keep their distance from the unsavory-looking duo. When they arrived at the roundhouse, the two hoboes unrolled their respective bundles of paper and spread them out on some workmen's carts before sitting down. No knives; just paper to sit on! On another occasion, Merylo ac-cidentally blundered on to Republic Steel property and found himself "arrested" by company police. Although he makes light of the whole incident in his report, a shabbily dressed Merylo obviously had a very difficult time convincing a couple of company guards that he was a real policeman from Cleveland, Ohio. On yet another occasion, a foul odor very reminiscent of a decomposing body turned out to be nothing more suspicious than a pile of corn and wheat that had been swept from a boxcar and had later fermented in the rain.

On August 5, someone in the Cleveland Police Department phoned Youngstown with the unsettling news that Frank Vorell's father lay gravely ill. The two men immediately returned to Cleveland. The next day, Merylo concluded his official report on his odyssey among the transients. "I returned to this Office at 9:00 this A.M. and completed my duty reports, from July 13, 1940 to this date, August 6, 1940." In the last analysis, the two detectives had learned very little and accomplished even less. The undercover mission would never be repeated. What began on such a high note of expectation ended with barely a whimper.

—

On the morning of Saturday, November 2, 1940, Mike Seman of West Pittsburg was hunting rabbits at the edge of the swamp when he made a sickening discovery of a kind that had become all too common in that area over recent years—a human skull lying against a log. He alerted Constable Bannon, a veteran of all the local Pennsylvania killings stretching back to 1925, who then passed on word of the find to the state police, District Attorney Lamoree, and Coroner Nugent. As officials gathered at the discovery site, they soon found a male skeleton, on its back and covered with small logs, about forty-two feet away from the skull. The ground directly beneath the bones showed clear signs of a fire. Like the three bodies found in freight cars on May 3, 1940, this man was fairly short—about five feet six inches in height. Most of his teeth contained fillings, raising the admittedly slim possibility that he could be identified through his dental work. According to the *New Castle News* of November 2, Nugent remained vague about the time of death, placing it at about two months before the body's discovery, during cold weather. The head had been expertly removed with either a saw or a knife. As the small gathering of lawmen scanned the area, they had the unnerving feeling of having been through all of this before. After all, just over a year earlier, on October 19, 1939, the body of another man—still unidentified—had been found in the swamp a mere 150 yards away.

Predictably, word of the latest discovery was dutifully sent to Cleveland, but considering the veritable army of investigators the city had sent in 1939 and 1940 and the high-level meetings held during the earlier investigations among officials of so many Ohio and Pennsylvania municipalities, Cleveland's response this time hardly rose to the level of a "Ho-hum." Only two Cleveland officers drove to New Castle, Sergeant James Hogan, head of homicide, and Detective Emil Musil. Musil was one of the longest-serving veterans of the torso murders in Cleveland, and he had been on the scene where the first two of the Butcher's officially recognized victims had been found on September 23, 1935. By this point, however, if the surviving paperwork on the case can be taken as indicative of his role in the investigation, he had been pushed very much to the fringes. As for Hogan, as head of homicide he obviously had been involved in the investigation most of the time, but his involvement was nowhere near as deep as that of Merylo and Zalewski. It would seem that the top echelons of Cleveland's law enforcement community had definitely lost interest in the Pennsylvania murder-dismemberments.

The true reason for this tepid response from the Cleveland Police Department cannot be determined so long after the fact, but it may have had something to do with David Cowles's subsequent tests of the recovered vertebrae of the boxcar victims in 1939 and 1940, as well as the results of Normand Hoerr's examination of the same three victims at the Western Reserve University Medical School. Perhaps these further in-depth studies revealed details that pointed away from the Cleveland Butcher, despite Merylo's ongoing conviction that all the murders were related. We are unlikely ever to know for sure, but whatever the reason, Cleveland had lost interest in what had been going on in western Pennsylvania and was quietly closing the book. Musil's and Hogan's brief visit to New Castle in November 1940, therefore, probably should be seen as nothing more significant than a courtesy call.

—

A similar scenario played out once again a little more than six months later, when, on May 26, 1941, Albert H. Smoot and John Omuska hopped off a freight train in Aliquippa, Pennsylvania, only to stumble upon a man's leg, severed at the hip, resting on the bank of the Ohio River near the Sewickley Bridge. Detectives Sam Graham and Lester Leonard of Allegheny County ruled out the possibility that the disarticulated limb could have been sliced from the body by a steamboat paddlewheel, and since the discovery site was relatively close to the P&LE Railroad— which also ran by the New Castle–West Pittsburg Murder Swamp and into Kingsbury Run in Cleveland—both men immediately, though tentatively, connected the find specifically to the three Stowe Township butcheries of May 3, 1940, and the torso murders in general. Five days later, yet another limb turned up. William Kraus and Eugene Lewicki were rowing on a channel of the Ohio River north of Pittsburgh and near Neville Island and Coraopolis, Pennsylvania, when they found a second human leg floating near the Neville Coke Company. County detectives thought both limbs had come from the same body, and the new discovery immediately sparked more speculation about the torso murders in both Ohio and Pennsylvania. Merylo's request to follow up on the grim discoveries in Pittsburgh was readily granted by his superiors. Interestingly, perhaps significantly, he met up and conferred with Sergeant Samuel J. Riddle, one of the first officers on the scene in Stowe

Township to investigate the triple horror of May 3, 1940. But here the trail goes cold. Merylo's files contain no follow-up reports on the two severed legs; nor does he mention them in his memoirs. Moreover, any official paperwork in Allegheny County detailing a formal examination of the limbs at the coroner's office has disappeared.

—

Until the day he died, Peter Merylo was haunted by the idea that the answer to the torso murders in both Ohio and Pennsylvania lay hidden somewhere along the railroad lines between Cleveland and New Castle, among the dispossessed who gathered around the Youngstown incinerator and huddled together in makeshift camps, in the debris of abandoned hobo jungles, in the desolation of Kingsbury Run and the impenetrable darkness of Murder Swamp. In the later phases of his investigation, he was drawn to potential suspects who either worked on the railroads or simply rode them. In 1939, Edward H. Fritz, a *New Castle News* reporter, alerted Merylo to a railroad worker of mixed African American and Mexican heritage, but this tantalizing lead, like so many others, simply led nowhere. In 1942, information about George William Piersol, a railroad conductor living in Cleveland, was passed on to Merylo by Captain Fasoles of the Pennsylvania Railroad Company. The initial tip had come from Piersol's supervisor, Robert Burk Kiggins, who had reported that the suspicious conductor carried a satchel of medical instruments and was "mentally deranged." But the mysterious Mr. Piersol passed from Merylo's radar screen as quickly as he had appeared. Merlyo's frustration had grown to such a degree that he briefly considered a suspect that simply defied logic, especially when judged by the light of his own personal profile: a man with a peg leg. No one with a disability that serious could possibly have been responsible for the murders in either Cleveland or Pennsylvania. The bodies of Cleveland's first two officially recognized victims had been carried, one at a time, down a sixty-foot slope known as Jackass Hill—a feat of strength and physical dexterity far beyond someone with a wooden limb. Moreover, such an individual could hardly pass through the dilapidated Kingsbury Run area or the Pennsylvania railroad yards without attracting attention. Also, negotiating the treacherous Murder Swamp would be impossible for someone so severely incapacitated.

A man hobbled by such a disability would necessarily stick in the memories of those who saw him, but there were never any reports in Cleveland or Pennsylvania, official or anecdotal, of someone with a peg leg. Finally, although forensic science may not have been then what it is today, police certainly would have noticed something as obvious as a series of round depressions in the ground at the crime scenes.

In both his final police report, dated March 15, 1943, and his two memoirs, Merylo outlines and recommends a detailed plan for continuing the investigation. He envisioned four two-man teams working underground and composed of men willing to undergo the hardships he and Frank Vorell had endured during their three-week odyssey in 1940. These hand-picked men, he stated, should dress as transients and ride freight trains from one city to the next. They should not work in pairs, he cautioned, but separately—yet close enough to keep an eye on each other should trouble arise. One of his recommendations betrays his attitude toward the targets the Butcher seemed to favor. "They [the two-man teams] should be able to recognize a pervert when one appears in the vicinity where the Torso victims were found. This pervert may be the next victim, he should be watched from a distance to see who would become friendly with him." Merylo recommended the cost of this strategy be borne equally by both Ohio and Pennsylvania. Nothing, of course, ever came from Merylo's grandiose plan.

NOTES

Frank Dolezal remains the only man arrested and charged in the torso murders. He was arrested by agents of Cuyahoga County Sheriff Martin L. O'Donnell in July 1939, but the flimsy case against him began to deteriorate almost immediately. Six weeks after his arrest, Dolezal was found hanging in his cell. Coroner Gerber's official ruling of suicide has been questioned ever since that judgment was handed down in August 1939. In *Though Murder Has No Tongue: The Lost Victim of Cleveland's Mad Butcher* (Kent State University Press, 2010), I argue that Frank Dolezal's death was most likely murder. Patrolman Frank Vorell's sister Louise was married to Frank Dolezal's younger brother Charles. Vorell was, therefore, related to Frank Dolezal by marriage.

As I indicated in the text, the documentation of this particular chapter in the torso murder investigation is by far the most detailed. Merylo discussed his and Vorell's undercover activities extensively in both sets of memoirs, while his report, at nearly ten thousand words, minutely covers their movements and experiences day by day. As noted previously, whenever discrepancies arose between the memoirs and the sixteen-page, single-spaced report, I took the latter as the more reliable, it having been written immediately after the events being covered.

Interestingly enough, Merylo does not mention in either set of memoirs his harrowing plunge into the smoldering muck during his undercover exploration of the swamp. The only documentation of this particular occurrence appears in Paul McClung's article in the July 1952 issue of *Front Page Detective.*

The material I used concerning the last officially recognized Pennsylvania victim, found in November 1940 was drawn from the *New Castle News.* The discovery of the two single legs in May 1941 was covered by the *Pittsburgh Sun-Telegraph* and the *Pittsburgh Press.*

As stated in the text, Merylo's plan for continuing the investigation appears in both his memoirs and in his final report, which he submitted upon retiring from the Cleveland Police Department in March 1943.

CHAPTER 6

"MY NAME IS LEGION, FOR WE ARE MANY"

It is not my intention in this book to offer a positive identification of the Mad Butcher of Kingsbury Run or to even speculate on who he may have been. I dealt with that question in considerable depth in two earlier books, *In the Wake of the Butcher: Cleveland's Torso Murders* and *Though Murder Has No Tongue: The Lost Victim of Cleveland's Mad Butcher.* My purpose here is twofold: to determine exactly how many murder-dismemberments occurred in Ohio and Pennsylvania between 1921 and 1950 and to examine whether Cleveland's Butcher, whoever he may have been, was responsible for all those deaths.

The two questions I ask here are not easy to answer. Several factors make such determinations extraordinarily difficult, occasionally reducing me to simply making educated guesses. The lack of surviving official paperwork remains the major stumbling block. As John Flynn, an assistant to Eliot Ness, learned to his surprise during his New Castle sojourn in the mid-1930s, officials had kept no formal documentation on any of the Murder Swamp victims, save for some random notations at the sheriff's office. This regrettable state of affairs leaves the modern researcher with a very sparse trail indeed—only the contemporary newspaper coverage and the possibly faulty memories of New Castle authorities. The record was somewhat more complete for the Pennsylvania boxcar butcheries of 1939 and 1940; the autopsy protocols still exist as do other pieces of formal documentation, including a detailed police report from one of the first officers on the scene in Stowe Township on May 3, 1940. Nevertheless, some very significant and important documents have simply been swallowed by time; all of the paperwork documenting the studies of human remains carried out at the Western Reserve Medical School has, unfortunately, been lost. The evidence available on the Cleveland killings that took place between 1934 and 1950 is much more complete. Despite the effects of the Great Depression, Cleveland at the time the torso murders began remained a major population center and a ranking industrial power. Both its police department and coroner's office were more or less state of the art for the day. The autopsy protocols and related documents from the coroner's office survive intact, and many random police reports—primarily Peter Merylo's—also have been preserved.

Even where records have been preserved, however, differences in the investigators' skills, equipment, and goals impede useful comparisons by the modern researcher. Ohio's Cuyahoga County had two different coroners during the years of the murders, A. J. Pearce and Samuel Gerber, and different pathologists performed the formal procedures, not only in Cleveland but in Pittsburgh, as well. Moreover, the quality and thoroughness of the autopsies varied considerably. The bodies found in Murder Swamp, for example, received far-less-skilled handling than those found in Cleveland; what passed for a formal autopsy in New Castle, Pennsylvania, was performed by an undertaker or a physician. Although everyone involved was a scientist of some stripe, seeking to produce an objective report, different individuals strove to be objective in different ways. One man's objectivity is not necessarily another's. In fact, that very objectivity is often a problem. In an autopsy protocol, a pathologist usually limits himself to describing what he sees, avoiding any speculation as to what may have led to what he is observing. Such discrepancies of method and objective can make it difficult to compare documents from two different observers when searching for similarities in the character of the dismemberments or in the killer's methods. Although he could occasionally be a bit sloppy, especially toward the end of his Cleveland career, the Mad Butcher performed his dismemberments and decapitations with the skill of a practiced surgeon. In every Pennsylvania case that involved decapitation, the pathologist of record noted precisely at what point in the neck the murderer had removed the head but did not necessarily comment on the nature of the wounds at the point of separation. Were the cuts clean or sloppy? Were there any hesitation marks? Was there any evidence of sawing or hacking? The lack of a common basis for comparison makes it difficult to draw conclusions about the killer or killers.

It is possible, however, to look at the surviving evidence from all the murders that have been attributed to the Mad Butcher through the lens of our contemporary understanding of serial killers and their methodology. Thanks to the pioneering work of modern profilers such as Robert Ressler and John Douglas, the dynamics of the serial killer personality and the characteristics of the crimes have been minutely analyzed and extensively documented. Today, an informed investigator dealing with a serial killer considers such issues as evidence of an organized or disorganized perpetrator, evolution of technique over time, victim preference, manner of death, control over both victim and crime scene, weapon or weapons of choice, comfort zones, and cooling off periods. None of these tools were available to the authorities during the thirty-year period of the Pennsylvania-Ohio murders. The standard investigative assumption at the time of the torso killings was that an individual was murdered by a family member or an acquaintance for understandable reasons: anger, jealousy, or greed. The term *serial killer* did not yet exist, and no one in law enforcement had even a minimal understanding of the motivations of a probable psychopath murdering and mutilating people he most likely did not know for his own murky reasons. Contemporary investigators had, of course, heard of such infamous killers from the past as Jack the Ripper and H. H. Holmes, but the psychological motivations behind their crimes were not fully understood.

For Peter Merylo, any killing involving a decapitation or a dismemberment of any kind, whether in Ohio or Pennsylvania, was enough to warrant inclusion in the Butcher's official tally. Others in law enforcement were not so sure: John Flynn expressed serious doubts that the bodies found in Murder Swamp were victims of Cleveland's Butcher; David Cowles was open-minded but characteristically reticent; and Eliot Ness remained utterly silent. In 1940, however, the newspapers in Ohio and Pennsylvania tended to accept Merylo's judgment; for an obvious reason, they jumped all over the sensational notion of an insane killer operating for decades over a two-state area and littering the landscape with dismembered and decapitated corpses: it made a good story. Recently, some commentators have tended to cast Merylo in the role of a well-meaning buffoon—a skilled and dedicated investigator, perhaps, but a man obsessed; a cop jumping on every lead no matter how questionable, charging through and ransacking the filth and decay of a major industrial city crippled by the Great Depression in a desperate search for clues; a man so wedded to his notions about the case and the perpetrator—and more than willing to share them with the press—that he couldn't, or wouldn't, accept any other possibilities. When Peter Merylo joined the Cleveland Police Department in 1919, new officers received no formal training. Each new officer was given his uniform, his gun, and his beat, and he was left to develop his professional skills, his gut instincts, and his street-wise savvy from day-to-day, on-the-job experience. Merylo had the best arrest record in the Cleveland Police Department when he retired, and Chief of Police Matowitz assigned him full-time to the torso murders in September 1936 because of his impressive record and his talents as an investigator. Merylo, however, seems to have been a curious combination of the impulsive and the methodical. He may have been quick to jump on an idea or a lead, but, once having made the decision to act, he approached his elected task in a thoughtful, carefully considered manner. He was not a forensic CSI scientist, nor a modern FBI profiler; he was a Depression-era cop molded by all the assumptions and armed with the investigative skills that defined law enforcement in those days. His most serious professional failing remained his knee-jerk reaction to any murder involving dismemberment or decapitation. In his later police reports, however, written before his retirement in March 1943, Merylo began to demonstrate that he was at least aware that it made a difference if someone were beheaded with a saw or a cleaver rather than the Butcher's knife.

Today, once having identified a potential suspect, it is fairly easy to see to what degree that individual matches the serial killer profile. His or her background can be pulled apart in a search for the standard traits and markers of the serial killer, including high intelligence, abuse or neglect in childhood, psychiatric or alcohol problems in the family, a previously low-level criminal activity such as setting fires and vandalism, evidence of bed-wetting as a child, and an overpowering fantasy life. Working the other way around—that is, trying to derive a portrait of the killer from an analysis of the crime scenes and everything else connected to the murders—is more difficult. Unfortunately, in this case, no other way is open.

—

In an article titled "The Fiend Has a Thousand Eyes" appearing in the July 1952 issue of *Front Page Detective,* Paul McClung provides a breakdown of all the victims attributed to the Cleveland Butcher up to that time. Since the article was written with Peter Merylo's help (and received his unqualified approval), it can only be assumed that this enumeration reflects the detective's thinking as of the date of publication; and, in light of the fact that no other listing was published before Merylo died in May 1958, the 1952 breakdown must represent his final tally of the Butcher's victims: fourteen in Cleveland, eleven in New Castle, three in Youngstown, three in Pittsburgh, and two in New York. Although the assertion that there were fourteen victims in Cleveland should not be accepted with one hundred percent certainty (official wisdom holds that there were only twelve), it remains a potentially accurate, certainly defensible position. The article's tally of eleven victims in New Castle (and West Pittsburg) is inaccurate, however; while the figures from Youngstown, Pittsburgh, and New York are at best highly questionable and at worst completely bogus. The inaccurate numbering of victims outside Cleveland actually begins in Merylo's memoirs, but since they were never published and no one apart from his family, his collaborator Frank Otwell, and perhaps a few close friends ever saw them, they are not the source of the article's fallacious figures. Those inaccuracies most likely stem from Merylo's subsequent public statements, the lack of formal documentation at the time some of the killings occurred, poor memories, and outright confusion. The only way to straighten out this tangle and arrive at an accurate body count is to consider in turn every murder victim between 1921 and 1950 that was ever attributed to the Mad Butcher.

THE EARLY NEW CASTLE AND PITTSBURGH MURDERS: 1921–1925

March 16, 1921
The murder of Emma Jackson on her family farm in Wampum, Pennsylvania, south of New Castle. Neck deeply slashed but head attached.

July 11, 1923
The torso of an unidentified six-year-old girl, found in the Beaver River, south of New Castle. Head and extremities never recovered; victim never identified.

October 1, 1923
The decapitated body of Charles McGregor, discovered in a woman's dressing room at one of Pittsburgh's municipal swimming pools along the Monongahela River. Head found later the same day.

February 11, 1924
Partial remains of an unidentified white male, found in a freight car sitting idle in Weirton Junction, West Virginia.

January 1, 1925
The charred torso of a young boy, found north of Ellwood City in the ruins of a burned shack. Head and extremities never recovered; victim identified as Luigi Noschesi.

The murders of Emma Jackson and the two children occurred around New Castle, Pennsylvania, but despite that geographic proximity, these three murders were clearly isolated events, unrelated either to the Kingsbury Run murders in Cleveland or to any of the subsequent Pennsylvania killings whose victims were found in New Castle's Murder Swamp or the derelict boxcars around Stowe Township. Emma Jackson was a seventy-three-year-old woman murdered in her own home. Moreover, news accounts at the time suggested sexual assault as the motive. None of these circumstances even remotely fit the MO of the Cleveland Butcher. He never killed anyone that old, nor did he ever murder in the victim's residence and leave the body behind. Finally, although sexual perversion apparently played a role in some of the Cleveland killings (victims 1 and 2 had been emasculated), outright sexual assault was not part of the Butcher's style.

Neither of the two unsolved cases involving children is connected to the subsequent murders committed in Cleveland or Pennsylvania, although there is a distinct possibility that they may be related to each other. Unlike the majority of serial killers, the Cleveland Butcher crossed both gender and racial lines, but he never killed any children. These two murder-mutilations were committed in the same geographic area a little less than eighteen months apart, and both young victims had been dismembered and decapitated in the same manner. None of the missing body parts in either case were ever recovered. All of this may suggest a seriously deranged and extremely violent pedophile, but not the Mad Butcher of Kingsbury Run.

Even though authorities were never able to prove it conclusively, the notion that Charles McGregor and the unidentified man, parts of whom were found in Weirton Junction, were somehow linked remains attractive and plausible. At the time of the two killings, police were struck by the similarity of the MOs and the proximity in both time and place of the killings. Some of the details of the McGregor murder—the sheer violence, the obvious rage, and the discovery of his body in a swimming pool changing room out of the season—could suggest a sexual encounter gone horribly awry, but there is simply no way to know. These two murders, however, don't seem to have been lumped in with those of the Murder Swamp victims of New Castle or the boxcar victims of Stowe Township—at least not at the time those later murders occurred. News of the 1923 murder of Charles McGregor had, indeed, been picked up by the *New Castle News*. But by the time Cleveland officialdom showed interest in the Pennsylvania butcheries in 1937, the entire focus was on Murder Swamp; the fourteen-year-old murder and decapitation in Pittsburgh had apparently been forgotten. Though McGregor is never identified by name in any of the more recent tabulations of Ohio-Pennsylvania torso victims, the addition of those two Pittsburgh murders of 1923 and 1924 to the Butcher's supposed tally could account for some the obviously inflated totals that have appeared in more recent years.

In 1939, Merylo added the unsolved murder of Emma Jackson to his final total of killings in both states. When he and other Cleveland officials visited New Castle on October 6, 1939, on the occasion of the discovery of Pennsylvania victim 6, Merylo spoke with *New Castle News* reporter Edward H. Fritz, a sportswriter with a consuming interest in local murders. Fritz not only passed on information about his own preferred suspect in the death of Emma Jackson—the railroad worker of mixed African American and Mexican descent—but assured Merylo that Jackson's unsolved murder had to be linked to those that followed. Fritz stated the killing took place in 1922. He was off by a year; she was murdered in 1921. He also incorrectly maintained that the unfortunate woman had been decapitated, although the newspaper reports published at the time—in March 1921—make no mention of decapitation, instead stating that Jackson's throat had been deeply slashed with either a straight razor or a long knife. Such is the role of faulty memory in human affairs! Another aspect of Jackson's death, the proximity of the B&O's railroad line to her family's farm, may partly explain how Merylo came to regard the railroads as playing a central role in the murders in both states.

It would seem that in the years leading up to the publication of McClung's article in 1952, Merylo was also adding the death of one or the other of the dismembered children—either the unidentified six-year-old girl or the boy thought to be fourteen-year-old Luigi Noschesi—to the Butcher's total, even though he never refers to them specifically. The two Pittsburgh killings of 1923 to early 1924 don't seem to have factored into Merylo's thinking. Admittedly, it remains somewhat difficult to be certain, but he never mentions Charles McGregor by name anywhere in his official reports, memoirs, or letters; nor is there any reference to the Weirton Junction murder. When Merylo wrote or dictated his undated memoirs sometime after his retirement, he put the Pennsylvania body count at twelve instead of the officially recognized ten. Either his memory was betraying him or he was adding at least two of the five victims from the early 1920s to the total of Pennsylvania killings that took place between 1925 and 1942. By the time Cleveland authorities became involved in the investigation of the New Castle killings in 1937, any local memories of the three Pennsylvania cases in and around that city from the 1920s would have been extremely vague, and if any of the specifics were remembered at all, they probably would have blurred and run together, passing, in the minds of most New Castle residents, including the police, into folklore and legend. Yet the new cases of decapitation and dismemberment probably stirred these dim memories, prompting New Castle authorities to share them with the Cleveland investigators, especially Merylo. It is even conceivable that over time the cases of the six-year-old girl whose body was found in 1923 and Luigi Noschesi in 1925 had collapsed into a single event, thus explaining how Merylo arrived at the figure of twelve Pennsylvania victims. By 1952, however, he had lowered his tally of bodies found in the New Castle–West Pittsburg area to eleven. Obviously, he had had second thoughts about something and was adjusting his total accordingly, though he was still obviously including Emma Jackson.

Jackson's murder, however, shares with the other murders counted even fewer characteristics than those of the children. Her 1921 murder, on the Jackson farm in Wampum, Pennsylvania, was clearly an isolated event with one or more suspects on the scene: a black man who came to Emma Jackson's door the day before she was killed and the same or another black man seen leaving the family farm around the time of her death. (It is unclear whether this was one man or two.) The two Pennsylvania children killed, decapitated, and dismembered in 1923 and 1925 respectively may have been the work of a single, deeply disturbed and violent predator, but this killer obviously was not the same individual who slashed Emma Jackson's throat. Likewise, the two Pittsburgh murders could be the work of the same individual, but that man was clearly not responsible either for the Jackson murder or the terrible murders of the two children. At least three, possibly as many as five, perpetrators were responsible for these horrible murders in the New Castle–Pittsburgh area during the early 1920s, but not one of them was the Mad Butcher of Kingsbury Run.

THE NEW CASTLE MURDER SWAMP VICTIMS: 1925-1934

October 6–8, 1925
The decapitated body of an unidentified white male found in the New Castle Murder Swamp. Head found by police two days later; victim never identified.

October 17, 1925
Headless skeleton of a large male found in the New Castle Murder Swamp. Head never found; victim never identified.

October 19, 1925
Female skull discovered in the swamp. Rest of body never recovered; victim never identified.

These three bodies, discovered within two weeks of one another, form the infamous triple mystery of October 1925. They are the first three of the five officially recognized Murder Swamp victims. Of the three, the first remains the most interesting. The headless corpse had been jammed into the depression under the roots of a storm-felled tree, an action suggesting rage and retaliation, as well as an attempt to hide the corpse. The head had been buried beneath the feet. Initially, the scene appears to anticipate elements associated with Cleveland's first four officially recognized murder victims. The heads of the first two had been similarly buried (see below, September 23, 1935–June 6, 1936). A closer look, though, revealed that the differences far outweighed the similarities. The Cleveland Butcher displayed his first four victims in various ways; the perpetrator or perpetrators in New Castle were obviously trying to hide the body. Likewise, while Cleveland's butcher had buried the heads of his first two victims in such way so as to ensure the police would find them, the head of the first Murder Swamp corpse had been hidden completely.

As for the other two partial corpses discovered in Murder Swamp in October 1925, so little documentation on their cases has survived that it is simply impossible to say whether these murders (if that is what they actually were) are related either to the Cleveland murders or the other western Pennsylvania killings. Without documentation, there is nothing to indicate that the victims had actually been decapitated: the remains were skeletal, and since contemporary coverage makes no mention of knife marks on the bones, there is nothing either to confirm or confute the heads simply fell off as the bodies decomposed and the bones were dispersed by animals.

Considering the existing evidence and applying current knowledge of how serial killers operate, it seems highly unlikely that the three Murder Swamp victims of October 1925 were the work of the Cleveland Butcher; it would be another ten years before killings began in Cleveland. Serial killers have been known to become inactive in their violent careers for a variety of reasons, the most common being military service, incarceration of some sort, or hospitalization. But a ten-year sabbatical in the early years of his activity, coupled with a complete change in the manner of disposal—the Murder Swamp victims were hidden, the Cleveland victims were left in the open—would be exceedingly rare. When Cleveland authorities profiled the Butcher in September 1936 at a special conference called by then-coroner A. J. Pearce, one point the attendees agreed on was his knowledge of Kingsbury Run, the Cleveland Flats, and the adjacent areas. The Butcher knew the Run well enough to move through it at night while avoiding detection. It simply strains credulity to assume that the same person could have an equally intimate knowledge of New Castle's Murder Swamp, an area known only to locals and one far more remote and difficult to traverse than its Cleveland counterpart.

October 15, 1934
The badly decomposed, partly buried corpse of a man discovered on the south-western edge of the Murder Swamp close to West Pittsburg. Body intact; victim never identified.

This body clearly was not the work of Cleveland's Butcher. The man had not been decapitated. Most significantly, the Butcher always removed the heads of his victims, a gruesome indignity that more than anything else remains his trademark, his signature. Although most of the victims that can be attributed to him were further dismembered, in a few instances, decapitation remained the sole act of mutilation. Moreover, this 1934 body found near West Pittsburg had been partly buried. The Butcher never buried his victims. In many cases, he casually disposed of the pieces simply by leaving them on the ground or dumping them in the Cuyahoga River or Lake Erie. In the few instances that he did hide part of a victim, he did so in such a way so as to ensure its eventual discovery and guarantee a shock. The repeal of Prohibition in 1933 does not preclude this victim being a casualty of the bootleg wars or other forms of mob violence; distilling bootleg hooch and avoiding the liquor tax was still cheaper than legally producing potent potables. It is significant, however, that the dumping of bodies in Murder Swamp slowed markedly after the repeal of Prohibition.

Since no reports of missing persons had been filed in the immediate area of New Castle, Ellwood City, and West Pittsburg, Pennsylvania, local authorities and the press ultimately inclined toward the conclusion that all these murders were the work of bootleggers operating out of either Youngstown, Ohio, or Pittsburgh, Pennsylvania, a conclusion supported by the level of mob violence in the region at that time. Moreover, Merylo and Vorell reported that the transients they approached in the area while the detectives were working undercover in July and August 1940 shared this opinion. Virtually all the Murder Swamp victims from this period had been hidden deeply in the sprawling tangle of trees, undergrowth, and marshland, making their discovery a one-in-a-thousand chance. The Cleveland Butcher, in contrast, hid nothing. He arranged some of his victims as if they were elements in a ghastly stage tableau; others he merely tossed away like trash. We can never be sure whether the Murder Swamp killings were the work of a single bootleg hit man or a group. It also would be foolish to rule out a killer or killers unrelated to the mob or to Cleveland's Butcher. Local mobsters were not the only assassins who regarded the dismal tangle of vegetation as the ideal spot to hide a corpse; an area so remote and impenetrable would obviously be attractive to any killer wishing to dispose of a body. This initial set of Murder Swamp victims could be the handiwork of as many as four different individuals or as few as one; there is simply no way to know. But, however many killers were involved, none of them was the Mad Butcher of Kingsbury Run.

THE CLEVELAND MURDERS: 1934-1950

September 5, 1934
The badly decomposed lower half of an unidentified woman's torso, thighs still attached, found along the shore of Lake Erie, east of Cleveland. Head never recovered: other parts of the body recovered during the next few days; victim never identified.

Called the Lady of the Lake by Cleveland investigators, this victim has always been the subject of debate as to whether she should be officially included in the Cleveland Butcher's tally. Cleveland's daily newspapers were decidedly split on the issue. An official list of torso victims published by the Cleveland Police Department in the late 1930s, however, accepts her as one of the Butcher's victims. At that time, she was designated as victim 0. The first piece of victim 7 would be found on February 23, 1937, in the same general area along the lake shore—a circumstance suggesting that both victims had been disposed of in a similar manner in the same location. The only factor arguing against her inclusion in the Cleveland cycle of torso murders remains the time element. The year that elapsed between the discovery of the Lady of the Lake and the finding of the first two officially recognized victims of Cleveland's Mad Butcher (at the base of Jackass Hill) represents an uncharacteristically long cooling off period for the Butcher. After the discoveries at Jackass Hill, bodies accumulated at fairly regular intervals for the next four years. It can be argued, however, that her murder may have been a violent response to a major stressor in the Butcher's life, a circumstance or series of circumstances that would not be repeated for another year. (It is also possible, although highly unlikely, there were other victims during this period that have remained undiscovered for almost eighty years.)

September 23, 1935
The naked, decapitated, and emasculated corpses of Edward Andrassy and an unidentified second man discovered at the base of Jackass Hill in Kingsbury Run, close to East 55th Street. The heads of both victims were recovered, but the second victim found was never identified.

These are the first two officially recognized victims of Cleveland's Mad Butcher. Although the unidentified man was killed first, Andrassy is generally considered victim 1 because his body was the first to be discovered. Considering the gruesome nature of the double murder, the reporting in the Cleveland press seems rather muted. That coverage, however, does provide a window onto an age when journalistic standards were rather different from those of today. The discovery had been made by two neighborhood boys, aged sixteen and twelve; the *Cleveland Press* not only printed their names and ages but their addresses and pictures as well. At this point, it is instructive to recall the October 1924 decapitation murder of Charles McGregor in the women's changing shack at one of Pittsburgh's municipal swimming pools. At a casual glance, there would seem to be undeniable links that could conceivably tie the murders of Edward Andrassy and Mc-Gregor together: both men had been decapitated, both bodies were naked save for a pair of socks, and the heads of both men were found buried in the ground. There are also glaring differences, however: McGregor had been killed where his body lay, while Andrassy had been murdered elsewhere and his body merely dumped where it was later discovered; there was blood all over the scene of the McGregor murder, while Andrassy's corpse had been drained of blood before disposal; and the decapitation of McGregor had been sloppy, while Andrassy's head had been removed with the skill of a trained surgeon.

January 26–February 7, 1936
The disarticulated pieces of a woman's corpse, discovered in two different locations on two different days. Although her head was

never found, she was later positively identified as Florence Polillo of Ashtabula.

Florence Polillo is officially designated as victim 3 in the cycle of Kingsbury Run murders.

June 5–6, 1936
The head and naked body of a male found in front of a railroad police building in Kingsbury Run, close to East 55th Street. Victim never identified.

This victim (no. 4) and the proceeding three are all clearly the work of Cleveland's Mad Butcher. In fact, these four remain the best known of all the victims attributed to him—partly because two of them were positively identified and partly because, taken as a group, these four cases define all the elements of his "style" so precisely. None had been murdered where their bodies were found. All four had been killed, decapitated, and their bodies stripped and drained of blood at some unknown, never-identified location. All four were found in the same relatively small geographic area, three of them in Kingsbury Run. There is also an obvious element of joking display associated with all four— the killer, not content with merely abandoning his victims, behaved like a twisted artist and took special care with the arrangement of each scene. The heads of Edward Andrassy and victim 2 had been buried in the ground, but in such a way as to ensure the police would find them. The first set of Florence Polillo's remains had been carefully wrapped in newspaper, neatly packed into two half-bushel produce baskets, covered with burlap bags, and left perched on the top of a snow bank behind a manufacturing building at East 20th Street and Central Avenue. The second set, however, had been merely dumped in a shallow depression in a different location. As for victim 4, his body had been left in the open, but his head had been neatly wrapped in his pants and deposited under a tree for the unwary to find. The discovery of this fourth official victim marked a turning point in the local history of the torso murders. In the early summer of 1936, the police were still regarding the killings as isolated events; beginning with victim 4, however, the police, the public, and city papers began to see the accumulated bodies as the work of a single perpetrator; hence, the coverage in the local press began to increase in intensity.

July 22, 1936
The nude, decapitated body of a white male about forty years of age, found on Cleveland's southwest side. Judged to have been murdered a month earlier. His head was recovered, but he was never identified.

The Butcher's fifth officially recognized Cleveland victim was discovered lying on his chest near the remnants of a camp fire. The dried blood on the ground suggested he had been killed and decapitated on the site where he was found. This is the only Cleveland victim to be found on the city's west side and the only one apparently killed where his body was discovered. These facts have led to questions in some quarters as to whether this victim was actually murdered by Cleveland's Butcher.

September 10, 1936
Part of a male torso discovered in a stagnant pool near East 37th Street in Cleveland. Head never found; victim never identified.

Though the entire body of victim 6 was never recovered, Cleveland police retrieved additional pieces from the filthy pool over the next month.

February 23, 1937–May 1937
The upper part of a woman's torso discovered along the shores of Lake Erie, east of Cleveland. The lower half found three months later near the downtown area. Head never recovered; victim never identified.

The cause of death for most of the Cleveland victims had been decapitation. Victim 7 was clearly an exception; she was already dead when the killer dismembered her body. The upper part of her corpse had washed ashore at virtually the same spot that the first recovered piece of the Lady of the Lake—later designated as victim 0—had been found in September 1934. This coincidence, along with the expert disarticulation, prompted the inclusion of this early Cleveland victim in the Butcher's tally.

June 6, 1937
Partial skeletal remains of a petite black woman discovered under the Lorain-Carnegie Bridge in Cleveland. Head discovered with the remains; victim tentatively identified as Rose Wallace.

This woman was dead for about a year when she was found, and there have been nagging questions as to her legitimacy as a victim of

Cleveland's Butcher, primarily because of her race. It is extremely rare for a serial killer to cross racial lines. The coroner's office, however, was sure she should be included in the Butcher's final tally.

July 6, 1937
Pieces of a male corpse pulled from the Cuyahoga River over a week's time. Head never recovered; victim never identified.

The discovery of this victim coincided with labor troubles in the steel industry severe enough to bring in the National Guard to keep order. After the first piece of the body had been pulled from the river, National Guard troops actually aided Cleveland police in the search for the rest of the corpse. The coroner's office noted that the Butcher's level of violence was increasing; the body had been far more badly mutilated than any previous victim.

April 8–May 2, 1938
Incomplete corpse of a young woman pulled from the Cuyahoga River. Head never recovered; victim never identified.

For the first time in the torso murder cycle, the coroner's office detected drugs in the corpse's system. However, since the woman's arms were never recovered, the coroner was unable to determine whether the killer had used the drugs to incapacitate his victim or the woman was simply an addict.

August 16, 1938
The badly decomposed pieces of a woman's body and the skeletal remains of a man discovered in a trash dump at East 9th Street and Lake Shore Road. Although the heads of both victims were recovered, neither victim was ever identified.

At the time, the press reacted to the same-day discovery of these two new Cleveland victims, designated 11 and 12, with predictable extravagance and fury. Not since September 23, 1935, had two bodies been found at the same time. In 1983, however, the legitimacy of counting the two bodies as victims of the Butcher would come into question. In that year, David Cowles sat down for an extensive interview with Florence Schwein (the first curator of the Cleveland Police Historical Society Museum) and police lieutenant Tom Brown to discuss his years in the Cleveland Police Department and the significant cases on which he worked. Cowles revealed that the woman designated as murder victim 11 was not a legitimate torso victim; her body had already been embalmed. This determination had been made by anatomist Dr. T. Windgate Todd of the Western Reserve University Medical School after the body parts were turned over to the school's anatomy department following the official autopsy. Yet the pathologist who had performed the original autopsy had judged the unidentified woman to be a victim of the Mad Butcher, even though he had been unable to determine the actual cause of death. With the status of victim 11 in doubt, what about the skeletal remains found in the same dump and labeled victim 12? The autopsy protocol on victim 12 contained nothing beyond apparent knife marks at the joints to tie the unidentified male to the Butcher's other murders. This incredible revelation of sloppiness in the coroner's office never made the daily papers. There can be no doubt, however, that David Cowles and the office of Safety Director Ness were aware of this major blunder, and this knowledge undoubtedly played a significant role in their handling of the three boxcar victims discovered on the same day in Pennsylvania's Stowe Township, influencing their decision in 1940 to bypass the coroner's office and turn over the boxcar victims' remains to the Western Reserve Medical School for further analysis. Should Cleveland victims 11 and 12 even be counted in the Butcher's total?

There is a noticeable curve, a step-by-step progression in the Butcher's style over the years in which the fourteen Cleveland victims were dispatched and found. After victim 4 was found in June 1936, he apparently lost interest in the taunting arrangement of bodies, heads, and dismembered limbs. The careful staging of the crime scenes observable in the earlier murders gives way in the later cases to a casual abandonment or simple dumping of body parts on the ground, in the Cuyahoga River, or in Lake Erie. Also, the precise cutting that informed the disarticulation of the earlier victims becomes more savage and somewhat sloppier as the body count increases.

July 22, 1950
The discovery near East 22nd Street of the decapitated and dismembered body of a man. Head recovered; victim later identified as Robert Robertson.

The disarticulated remains were found scattered around a pile of steel girders on the property of the Norris Brothers Company on Davenport

Avenue, near East 22nd Street, after company employees had become aware of a foul odor in the immediate area. City papers instantly jumped on the story, emphasizing the obvious similarities between Robertson and the twelve recognized victims of the Butcher from the 1930s. Coroner Gerber acknowledged the chilling echoes of the past raised by the Robertson killing but also pointed to the twelve-year gap that separated this murder from the others.

Gerber admitted that there were discernable differences in the disarticulations of some of the Cleveland victims, but he argued that these differences were slight and maintained that all the murder-dismemberments in the city were the work of the same individual.

After Cleveland victim 4 was found in June 1936, the Butcher apparently lost interest in the taunting arrangement of bodies, heads, and dismembered limbs in which he had indulged after his earlier killings. Pieces of the later victims seemed to have been merely tossed aside or dumped. Serial killers often mutate from organized to disorganized as their careers advance, and that pattern or curve is clearly discernable in the Cleveland murders.

—

As I stated at the beginning of this chapter, it is not my purpose in this book to speculate as to the identity of the Mad Butcher of Kingsbury Run. Here, my goals are to correctly determine the total number of victims killed in Ohio and Pennsylvania between 1921 and 1950 and to establish whether a single individual can be held responsible for all of them. Those questions, however, cannot be explored without examining Eliot Ness's so-called secret suspect. This suspect remains the lynchpin of Cleveland's investigation—the only man to ever receive serious consideration from the Ness office and the police—and though tales about this mysterious, unnamed individual had been part of torso murder folklore since the late 1930s, they were not verified until Cowles's 1983 interview with Schwein.

In May 1938, Ness operatives picked up a man about whom their suspicions had been steadily growing for some time: a once-promising physician—now hobbled by mental illness, alcohol abuse, and drug addiction—named Francis Edward Sweeney. Eliot Ness may have been a master at exploiting the local press to promote his actions and initiatives, but he also knew how to play his cards very close to his chest when he had to. Hence, the path that led him to Sweeney is buried under layers of secrecy more than seventy years old. Dr. Sweeney's cousin happened to be Martin L. Sweeney, the very colorful, locally prominent Democratic congressman from the twentieth district. Because of this family connection, Ness's subsequent handling of Francis had to be planned and executed under an impenetrable cloak of secrecy. Ness's men spirited Dr. Sweeney from the streets to a room in the old Cleveland Hotel (now the Renaissance) on Public Square, where they held him for at least a week, perhaps two. There Sweeney was grilled for eight hours a day every day by David Cowles and Dr. Royal Grossman, a psychiatrist working for Cuyahoga County. At some point during this marathon interrogation, Ness brought in Leonard Keeler, inventor of the modern-day polygraph and the reigning expert in its use, from Illinois. Keeler conducted at least one examination of Sweeney and assured Ness that the suspect was, indeed, the Butcher. Keeler's conclusion, however, was not enough to prosecute Sweeney; it is the learned opinion of an acknowledged expert in his field, but it is not an ironclad identification, and although there is ample circumstantial evidence to support Keeler's judgment (which is also for that matter, Eliot Ness's), there is nothing rock solid to substantiate it.

Nevertheless, any serious consideration of who may have killed whom in Ohio and Pennsylvania must begin with this conclusion that Sweeney was the Butcher; it cannot be downplayed, casually dismissed, or completely ignored, although some commentators on the case have tried. For those arguing that the same individual was responsible for all the horrors in both states, Keeler's identification of Sweeney as the Butcher looms as far more than a mere speed bump; it becomes an insurmountable impediment, since Sweeney could not have committed them all. His movements during the 1920s and most of the 1930s are easy enough to trace through Cleveland city directories and other public documents. He simply cannot be placed in western Pennsylvania at the precise moments that some of the murders occurred.

Conversely, Sweeney cannot be ruled out as a credible suspect for the murders in Cleveland. Eliot Ness was a careful, deliberate man who would have never undertaken an operation this complicated, sensitive, and expensive without far more to go on than vague, unsupportable suspicions or simple gut feelings. Ness operatives had been tracking the seriously deranged physician for some time. David Cowles had put together a secret undercover team of informants, made up of low-level hoods and police officers fresh out of the academy, who were able to operate in complete secrecy and reported directly back to him. Although surviving records do not state exactly how long this surveillance continued or how successful it was, Ness was not acting impulsively in ordering Sweeney's detention and interrogation. Ness would never have gone to the considerable expense and trouble of secretly bringing Leonard Keeler to Cleveland from the Midwest on nothing more than a hunch. Moreover, Keeler's expertise with the polygraph he had perfected and tested cannot be questioned or casually ignored. He was the best in the business, and if he declared Francis Sweeney to be the Butcher based on his tests, that opinion must be treated seriously and with respect. In order to dismiss Sweeney as the most viable suspect in the Cleveland murders, one must be willing to argue that a remarkably elaborate and secret operation, carefully planned and executed, had been formulated and carried out just for the heck of it; that those involved worked to keep the whole thing secret for four decades just for fun; and that several highly intelligent professionals (no doubt in possession of information since lost) simply got it all wrong. With nothing more solid to go on than an inadmissible lie detector test, Ness was forced to let Sweeney go after his grueling hotel room ordeal.

In August 1938, Sweeney successfully applied for admission to the Sailors' and Soldiers' Home in Sandusky, Ohio. From then until his death at the age of seventy in 1964, the derelict doctor was shuttled around to various institutions in the Veterans Administration system. He regarded Eliot Ness as his nemesis and even fired off an incoherent four-page letter to J. Edgar Hoover, complaining about Cleveland's former safety director. Sweeney amused himself further by bombarding Ness with a stream of cryptic, jeering postcards and letters in which he slyly hinted at his guilt in the murders without ever admitting anything. Finally declared legally incompetent by VA doctors in the mid-1950s, Sweeney ended his days in a psychiatric facility in Dayton, Ohio. (Additional information about Francis Edward Sweeney and his role in the torso murder investigation can be found in my two previous books on the case, *In the Wake of the Butcher: Cleveland's Torso Murders* and *Though Murder Has No Tongue: The Lost Victim of Cleveland's Mad Butcher.*)

—

In 1952, Merylo put the tally of Cleveland murders attributed to a single killer, the Butcher, at fourteen. Obviously, he is adding the Lady of the Lake from 1934 and Robert Robertson from 1950 to the officially accepted total of twelve Cleveland victims, and his conclusions are defensible. By 1939, Cleveland Police had accepted the former as a legitimate torso victim; an official list published by the department in that year included her in the Butcher's tally and designated her as victim 0. When Robert Robertson's disarticulated remains were discovered on the grounds of the Norris Brothers Construction Company in July 1950, city newspapers wrote ceaselessly of the familiar Kingsbury Run technique involving decapitation and dismemberment, and Samuel Gerber, Cuyahoga County's coroner, was inclined to agree—in part because there did not seem to be any alternative. I have seen the Robertson file in the Cleveland Police Department; and although the authorities followed up on several leads and pursued a number of potential suspects, including doctors, no viable candidate emerged. The only thing that bothered Gerber at the time was the lapse of twelve years between the discovery of the Butcher's last recognized victims in 1938, nos. 11 and 12, and the murder of Robertson in 1950. Gerber may not have known much about the dynamics of the serial killer mind, but a cooling off period of more than a decade did strike him as unlikely. Legitimate debate over the Robertson killing is likely to persist: was it part of the torso cycle or simply an isolated event? Merylo had retired from the police department in 1943, so he was not on board for the official investigation into Robertson's death. Everything he knew about it would have come to him secondhand, from newspaper accounts or through conversations with his old buddies in the police department. Merylo undoubtedly included the Robertson murder-dismemberment in his list of Butcher victims because virtually everything about the crime, from the disarticulation of the body to the random scattering of the parts, matched his style so closely. There is, however, a much more solid reason to attribute Robertson's murder to the Butcher—something Merylo probably did not know. In the weeks before the discovery of the body, Norris Brother employees watched a suspicious-looking man perform a daily ritual: he would mount a pile of girders, take off his shirt, and sunbath for several minutes. The description of the man they gave to police matched what Ness suspect Frank Sweeney would have looked like in 1950. At the time, the doctor was a resident of the Ohio Soldiers' and Sailors' Home in Sandusky, Ohio, but at that point, he could come and go as he pleased. It does not strain credulity, therefore, to argue that Robertson was, indeed, killed by the Butcher—Eliot Ness's suspect, Frank Sweeney. It is also possible to explain the discrepancies in the evidence concerning the victims from spring 1938 (nos. 11 and 12) by suggesting that while they may not actually have been killed by the Butcher, he may have been responsible for the disarticulation of their corpses. In considering such a scenario, one must again look at Sweeney. The doctor had interned at St. Alexis Hospital on Broadway and shared an office with Dr. Edward Peterka and four other physicians on the other side of the street. According to David Cowles in the 1983 interview, the Raus funeral home—responsible for handling the bodies of the unclaimed and indigent—stood next door. Sweeney enjoyed certain privileges at that establishment that allowed him to practice surgical techniques, and perhaps even dismemberment, on the unclaimed; it is entirely possible—even probable—that he disarticulated the dead bodies known as victims 11 and possibly 12 and deposited the remains in the dump at East 9th Street and Lake Shore Drive, a location in clear view from Eliot Ness's office, as a cruel joke to taunt the safety director. Merylo's tally of fourteen Cleveland victims for the Butcher is therefore defensible. While lingering questions and reasonable doubts will undoubtedly persist, particularly in light of the incomplete documentary record and of Cleveland officials' own clear doubts about the quality of the work coming out of the coroner's office, in the final analysis, there is no solid evidence contradicting the conclusion that Merylo's fourteen Cleveland victims, whether actually murdered or simply disarticulated, were the work of the same individual, the infamous Mad Butcher of Kingsbury Run.

THE LATER PENNSYLVANIA MURDERS: 1936-1940

July 1, 1936
The decapitated and decomposed body of a male found in a boxcar close to New Castle's Murder Swamp. Head never recovered; victim never identified.

This fifth officially recognized murder in the New Castle series was found less than a month after the discovery of Cleveland's victim 4. In fact, this victim was the only one to be killed in Pennsylvania while the Butcher's Cleveland rampage was in full swing. This timing, coupled with the fact that both bodies were found in places directly connected with the railroads, undoubtedly bolstered Detective Peter Merylo's developing belief that all the victims in both cities were murdered by someone who rode the rail lines. This particular victim, however, should be grouped with the later boxcar killings discovered in 1940.

October 13–19, 1939
Partly burned body of what appeared to be a young man found in Murder Swamp. Head recovered in a railroad gondola car six days later. Victim never identified.

This particular murder victim clearly does not belong in the Mad Butcher's tally. Someone had placed wads of paper in the hands of the corpse and set them on fire in an obvious move to frustrate any attempt to lift a set of fingerprints. The head had been tossed into a railroad gondola in a seeming attempt to simply dispose of it where no one was likely to find it. The killer probably assumed that after the rats and other scavengers had stripped the skull of flesh, it would be unrecognizable; perhaps he surmised that it would simply be covered over and lost in a load of coal or crushed by tons of scrap metal. In any case, the obvious goal was to prevent identification of the victim. The Cleveland Butcher never took such elaborate and obvious pains to keep his targets from being identified. He was perfectly content to allow victim 1, Edward Andrassy, and victim 3, Flo Polillo, to be identified through their fingerprints. Most of his other victims remained unidentified because the bodies were too badly decomposed upon discovery to get usable prints or because the prints lifted simply were not on file with any federal or state agency.

May 3, 1940
The discovery of three separate bodies in three different boxcars (part of a string of boxcars slated for demolition) on a railroad siding in Stowe Township, Pennsylvania. Two were male, one so decomposed its sex could not be initially determined. All three decapitated and two disarticulated at the hips and shoulders; some further mutilation.

None of the heads were recovered. Two bodies were never identified; the third body found identified as James Nicholson.

This triple find in a single place on a single day undoubtedly ranks as the most horrific and ghastly event in the three-decade history of the torso killings, far outstripping the double murder of Edward Andrassy and his unidentified companion in Cleveland on September 23, 1935. The sickening series of discoveries in a single morning produced an avalanche of press coverage in both Pennsylvania and Ohio and sparked high-level meetings and combined search efforts involving authorities from Cleveland, Youngstown, Pittsburgh, New Castle, and Butler.

The boxcar murders stand alone. They clearly are not connected with the bodies found in New Castle's Murder Swamp or with Cleveland's torso murders. In the Murder Swamp killings, the goal was to hide the bodies. All the victims had been at least partly buried or hidden in the depths of the area's tangled vegetation. In one case, someone had returned to the disposal site and heaped more twigs and leaves on the hidden corpse. In some instances, the murderer had gone further, deliberately trying to conceal the identity of the victim, as with the victim whose hands and fingers had been burned. In the Pennsylvania boxcar murders, no such attempts were made either to hide the bodies or to obscure the victims' identities. At that time, railroad cars were constantly in use; even derelict cars slated for demolition were routinely inspected. No one would dump a body in a railroad car and expect it to remain undiscovered forever. In the second discovery on May 3, 1940, the disarticulated body parts had been arranged in a pile, with the arms and legs on the bottom and the torso placed on top. As for James Nicholson—the third victim discovered that day—the killer had carved the word *Nazi* in his chest. All of this suggests either an attempt to send a message or a desire to shock. Whoever killed and butchered those railroad car victims knew the bodies would be found at some point.

Differentiating between Pennsylvania's boxcar victims and those found in or near Cleveland's Kingsbury Run is more problematic, since the two sets of murders share certain obvious characteristics. All three boxcar victims were naked and had been decapitated; the heads were never recovered; body parts were sometimes shoved into burlap bags; and although the killer did place the bodies in railroad cars, he made no attempt to hide them. All of these details recall elements of the Cleveland killings. Moreover, the piling up of arms, legs, and torso in the case of the second boxcar victim echoes the Butcher's "staging" of the bodies of his initial victims from late 1935 to mid-1936. Such seeming commonalities between the two sets of murder-mutilations may be misleading, however; it would be deceptively easy to make too much of them. There is nothing magical or even remotely special about burlap bags, for example; they were plentiful, readily available, extremely handy, durable, and just the right size for disarticulated human remains.

Moreover, the two sets of killings also display significant differences, the most compelling of which remains the instruments employed in decapitation. The Cleveland Butcher used a knife; whoever murdered and mutilated the Pennsylvania boxcar victims seems to have used a saw. Other differences exist as well. For one thing, the carving of the word *Nazi* on the chest of James Nicholson (the third boxcar victim) has no parallel in the Butcher's treatment of any of the Cleveland victims. For another, the Butcher disposed of his victims in the open while his Pennsylvania counterpart left his in railroad cars. Railroads may have been a common feature in both locales, but the Cleveland Butcher simply dumped some of his victims near the railroad lines; he never left one in a railroad car, nor, despite Merylo's contention in his memoirs, was there ever any evidence that he killed his victims in such cars. Of all the victims in Cleveland and western Pennsylvania, James Nicholson remains the only one to have obviously been killed in a railroad car. It remains highly unlikely that a killer would switch his weapon of choice and opt for a different disposal method simply because he had changed locales.

There has always been uncertainty as to exactly when and where the boxcar victims were killed. The available evidence seems to indicate that they had been murdered and mutilated long before the cars were moved from Struthers, Ohio, in late April 1940. (One of the victims even bore signs of having been frozen, suggesting death may have occurred as early as December 1939.) The fact that all three victims were discovered close together in the same string of derelict boxcars strongly suggests that the same person or persons were responsible for all three deaths—someone familiar with the layout of the railroad lines around Struthers and aware that these cars were out of service—perhaps a railroad worker. All of this points to a killer local to eastern Ohio or western Pennsylvania, not someone junketing from Cleveland. Similarly, the evidence in the Cleveland killings points to a local, someone intimately familiar with the sleazy joints, dives, and back alleys of the city. Neither Edward Andrassy nor Flo Polillo—the only Cleveland victims to be positively identified—had the remotest connection with the railroads; there is no report, official or anecdotal, that placed either of them anywhere near the railroad lines. They were city residents who haunted the seamier areas in and around the downtown. Andrassy's body had been dumped at the foot of Jackass Hill, close to the Shaker Rapid Transit tracks, but all the evidence points to him having been killed elsewhere. Flo Polillo lived in a run-down boarding house on Carnegie Avenue, and the two sets of her disarticulated remains turned up in the heart of the inner city. Whoever killed and decapitated Andrassy and Polillo was a Cleveland local, someone who lived in the same world they did, someone who regularly prowled the same sleazy bars and grimy streets; someone who may even have known them. Only a city resident well acquainted with Cleveland's dark alleys and hole-in-the-wall dives—not a Pennsylvania native working the railroads—would have had the local knowledge to prey on them there.

The strongest evidence against a link between the Kingsbury Run murders in Cleveland and the later Pennsylvania railroad killings remains the very obvious fact that Cleveland authorities lost virtually all interest in the Keystone State victims following the completion of Normand Hoerr's examination of the remains at the Western Reserve Medical School. History is not just a collection of statements made and events chronicled; history also comprises what did not happen. In this light, a careful look at the chronology of events after the discoveries of the three bodies in the boxcars on May 3, 1940, particularly the lack of an official Cleveland response to subsequent murders, strongly implies that authorities in Cleveland had ruled out a connection between their local butcheries and those in Pennsylvania.

The triple horror of May 3, 1940, in Stowe Township provoked a massive media storm. Newspapers in Cleveland and Youngstown, Ohio, and Pittsburgh and New Castle, Pennsylvania, rushed to capitalize on theories of a Mad Butcher reeking unimaginable carnage over a two-state area. William Randolph Hearst would have nodded with approval at the sensational, over-the-top coverage—an incredible, fascinating—indeed irresistible—tale of decomposing body parts and headless corpses, told in lurid prose and embellished with a full array of photographs. The discovery also spawned an equally impressive official response from the police departments of both northeastern Ohio and western Pennsylvania. Law enforcement agencies from all over the area joined forces with railroad police in a well-coordinated canvassing of railroad yards, sidings, and hobo camps—a hive of high-level activity minutely covered by an eager press establishment in both states. This hurricane of investigative fury culminated about two weeks later, when George Matowitz, Cleveland's chief of police, cabled Coroner Henney in Pittsburgh that he would be sending an undertaker to collect all three sets of remains and transport them to the Western Reserve University Medical School, where a carefully chosen pathologist, Dr. Normand Hoerr, would conduct his own examination.

The results of that examination have been either destroyed, discarded, or misplaced somewhere in the archival clutter of the Western Reserve Medical School, but the almost complete lack of any response from Cleveland's law enforcement community to subsequent murder-mutilations in western Pennsylvania certainly suggests, and suggests very strongly, that those results did not support a link between the boxcar murders and those in Cleveland—that, in Hoerr's opinion, the manner of dismemberment evident in the three boxcar victims did not match those in the Cleveland murders. There were hints of this conclusion even before Hoerr got his hands on those remains. David Cowles's examination of the neck vertebrae of one boxcar victim indicated that decapitation had been accomplished with some kind of saw rather than a large knife, the Mad Butcher's weapon of choice. The disappointing results of the Merylo's and Vorell's undercover foray into the hobo underworld during July and August 1940 undoubtedly also figured into official Cleveland's apparent judgment that the two sets of murders were not linked.

In November 1940, yet another victim turned up in the vicinity of New Castle, but this time, it prompted no massive response from Cleveland. David Cowles did not journey to Pennsylvania to learn more about this latest discovery, as he had in 1939 and May 1940. Instead, Sergeant James Hogan of the Homicide Unit and Emil Musil—neither of whom had been involved in the flurry of activity following the May 3, 1940, discovery—paid a simple courtesy call to New Castle. Cleveland officialdom made a polite nod—a "thank you, but no thank you"—to Pennsylvania authorities, but that was all. The city on the shore of Lake Erie was no longer interested in what was going on in the Keystone State.

Between May 26 and 31, 1941, still more remains surfaced: a pair of disarticulated male legs spotted in the Ohio River north of Pittsburgh. Despite some very brief speculation in the Pittsburgh press about a possible link to the Cleveland killings and the boxcar murders, Cleveland's police, once again, seemed uninterested. (See the epilogue for a full discussion of this discovery.) Peter Merylo's superiors granted his request to visit Pittsburgh for further investigation, but that permission seems to have been nothing more than a favor bestowed on a dedicated cop who was still plugging away at a case that had consumed him since the summer of 1936.

On June 21, 1942, the decapitated body of Ernest Alonzo turned up near Pittsburgh. (Again, see the epilogue for a full treatment of this murder.) This time, Pennsylvania authorities apparently didn't even bother to alert Cleveland to the discovery. Merylo seems to have found out about the murder on his own, though how is impossible to say. In an official police report written two months later, on August 17, he specifically asks for any sort of documentation concerning the latest Pennsylvania death. The four-page autopsy protocol was apparently sent to Merylo directly or, at the very least, turned over to him; Cleveland's only surviving copy is in his personal files.

November 2, 1940
Skull and skeleton of a male found in Murder Swamp, close to West Pittsburg. Victim never identified.

What was left of the body was lying on its back and had been covered with logs; evidence of a fire was clearly discernable beneath the skeletal remains. Obviously, the murderer had tried to destroy the corpse and then hide what was left. All of these details echo the treatment of earlier Murder Swamp victims, as distinct from the treatment of the Cleveland victims. When police in Cleveland learned of the discovery, only two officers were sent to consult with Pennsylvania authorities—a further indication that official Cleveland had decided there was no connection to the Kingsbury Run atrocities.

In 1952, Merylo inaccurately put the Pennsylvania body count at eleven instead of ten. As I indicated earlier, he is obviously including the unrelated 1921 murder of Emma Jackson in the Pennsylvania total, basing this decision purely on the mistaken belief of *New Castle News* reporter Edward H. Fritz that the elderly woman had been decapitated in a manner identical to the Cleveland victims. Merylo's assertion that there were three victims in Youngstown and three in Pittsburgh is likewise entirely false and no doubt results from simple confusion, although whose confusion is unknown. The total of ten Pennsylvania murders includes the three boxcar victims found on May 3, 1940, in Stowe Township. The railroad siding on which they were discovered stood close to Youngstown, and its police, as well as other authorities from that city, were deeply involved in the subsequent investigation. The formal autopsies of the remains, however, were performed in Pittsburgh. The three boxcar victims of Stowe Township are, therefore, apparently being counted three different times: once as part of the official Pennsylvania total of ten and twice more as a supposed trios of victims from Youngstown and from Pittsburgh.

THROUGH THE FOGS OF YESTERYEAR

One of the more significant and potentially enlightening events in the entire two-state murder-dismemberment saga occurred early in February 1940, when David Cowles suggested that Merylo and his partner, Zalewski, interview Eliot Ness's so-called secret suspect, Dr. Francis Edward Sweeney. Sweeney was staying at that time with his older sister on East 65th Street while his niece underwent an unspecified surgical procedure at nearby St. Alexis Hospital—ironically, the same hospital at which he had interned. In his official report of February 6, Merylo writes, "Dr. Sweeney was referred to us by Superintendent Cowles of the Scientific Bureau of Identification for a further check up, as it was believed that Dr. Sweeney might be a good suspect in the Torso Murders." This seemingly simple opening statement masks some very serious questions that, unfortunately, defy clear answers. This is the only surviving document recording a meeting between the lead investigator on the torso murders—hand-picked by Chief Matowitz—and Eliot Ness's prime—indeed, only serious—suspect, and it raises some very significant issues. How much did Peter Merylo know about Frank Sweeney? Did he know anything about the minutely planned and carefully executed hotel room interrogation that had taken place almost two years before? Was he even minimally aware that Sweeney was, or had ever been, a suspect? Merylo's phrase "for a further check up" clearly shows that this was not the first time the renegade physician had come under intense official scrutiny, but the phrase "was referred to us by Superintendent Cowles" strongly suggests that Merylo and Zalewski had not been involved in that prior investigation.

The inference to be drawn from this is quite clear, and the two lead investigators on the case had been kept out of the loop. This should not be read as an indication that Ness had doubts about Matowitz's crack team of detectives. It should rather been seen as a typical example of the safety director—comfortable working behind the scenes—taking advantage of the fact that the press saw Merylo and Zalewski as the public "face of the investigation," the pair to whom reporters invariably went for information, comments, and updates. The Merylo-Zalewski-press relationship created a smoke screen behind which Eliot Ness and David Cowles could work comfortably and in secret, the planning and execution of the hotel room interrogation being the best example. In other words, there were two separate investigations proceeding at the same time: one, the very public police efforts headed by Merylo and Zalewski; the other, a secret-behind-the-scenes probe led by Ness and Cowles. If Merylo was ignorant of Sweeney as a suspect and of Ness's investigation—and he apparently was—then Cowles's suggestion to the duo that they might want to interview Frank Sweeney reads as a shrewd bit of police work. He, Ness, and Leonard Keeler already had their opinion about Sweeney's guilt, at least in the Cleveland murders; what conclusions would two wholly independent investigators reach?

The two cops grilled Sweeney thoroughly, extracting information about many aspects of his past, including his education, his professional status, his alcoholism, and his family. They even elicited a firm denial from him that he had ever been to New Castle, Pennsylvania. While the substance of the interrogation was unremarkable, Merylo noted Sweeney's bizarre behavior throughout the interview; Sweeney paced up and down, answering questions as if he were dictating a business letter. Merylo concluded that the doctor suffered from a monstrously inflated ego, but, at the end of the day, he dismissed Sweeney as a viable suspect in the murders in both Cleveland and Pennsylvania. At this point, it must be remembered that Cowles had always been dubious about a Cleveland-Pennsylvania link; Merylo, on the other hand, was convinced that all the murders in both states had been committed by the same individual. Thus, his stated reasons for dismissing Frank

Sweeney as a viable suspect illustrate how deeply committed he was to his notion of a two-state, rail-riding Butcher.

> After our conversation with Dr. Sweeney, it is our opinion that Dr. Sweeney had no connection with the Torso Murders: due to the facts that he is not the type of person who would associate with perverts or other low type of characters. He is inclined to be delicate, even though he weights [sic] 220 pounds. He is not of the raw-boned type: and is rather fat and soft: he did not indicate he was of the outdoor type, and could not in our opinion fit into the type of person who would mix with the transients around the railroad tracks and swamps.

Based on the fact that Cowles was directly involved in the hotel room interrogation of Frank Sweeney and present when Keeler administered the polygraph examination and relayed his judgment about Sweeney's guilt to Ness, it is probably safe to assume he regarded Sweeney as the perpetrator of the Cleveland murders. But what about the Pennsylvania butcheries? Was the same person responsible for those as well? Could that perpetrator be Frank Sweeney? What did Cowles ultimately believe about a Cleveland-Pennsylvania connection? These are difficult questions to answer. History has recorded Cowles's actions — where he went and what he did — but has preserved few of his words and even fewer of his opinions. When Cleveland authorities first explored a possible connection between the Kingsbury Run murders and the Pennsylvania killings in late 1936 and early 1937, Cowles did not make the trip to New Castle. That particular honor went to John R. Flynn, an assistant to Eliot Ness, who expressed his doubts about any connection when he returned to Cleveland. At that point in time, however, Flynn had only the Murder Swamp victims to consider. Matters changed abruptly with the October 1939 discovery of another New Castle victim. Suddenly, Cowles was deeply involved, and suddenly, he was leading the local team to western Pennsylvania, collecting samples, and bringing them back for analysis in Cleveland.

The subsequent chronology of events is intriguing, if not entirely illuminating. Frank Sweeney had been interrogated in May 1938 and judged guilty by the inventor of the modern polygraph and the foremost expert in its use, Leonard Keeler. In August 1938, the last two of Cleveland's officially recognized twelve victims were found, and about a week later, Sweeney successfully petitioned for residency in the Ohio Soldiers' and Sailors' Home in Sandusky. The October 1939 discovery of yet another body in New Castle set off a flurry of activity in both states; four months later, Cowles alerted Merylo and Zalewski to Frank Sweeney, suggesting that they might want to interview him. Three months after this interview, railroad workers in Stowe Township found the Pennsylvania boxcar victims—three gruesomely murdered and dismembered transients whose remains had been dumped in a string of dilapidated boxcars awaiting destruction. That horrendous discovery prompted officials from five cities in the two-state area—Cleveland, Youngstown, Pittsburgh, New Castle, and Butler—to join forces in intense, coordinated action. And again, just as he had been present in New Castle in October 1939, David Cowles was the most prominent among the Clevelanders meeting in DA Park's office. Assuming he believed in Frank Sweeney's involvement in the Cleveland killings and remained at least dubious about a possible Pennsylvania link, just why was Cowles there? What did he believe at this point?

In 1938, Leonard Keeler had assured Ness and his associates, including Cowles, that his lie detector test pointed to Frank Sweeney as the notorious Butcher of Kingsbury Run; two years later, Merylo had dismissed him as a viable suspect for essentially one reason: he firmly believed that the same killer was responsible for the slaughter in both states, and he judged Frank Sweeney physically incapable of leading the arduous life of a rail-riding transient. The triple horror of May 3, 1940, no doubt raised at least momentary doubts in Cowles's mind. What if Merylo were mistaken? Although he had successfully applied for admission to the Sandusky Soldiers' and Sailors' Home in late August 1938, Sweeney could, theoretically, come and go as he pleased. He had not been formally declared incompetent by the Veterans Administration—at least, not yet. And though he was being watched by Ness's men, it is possible that he could have eluded his tails, slipped out of the facility, and indulged in a violent murder-dismemberment spree in neighboring Pennsylvania. Despite Merylo's dismissal of him, it remains possible that Frank Sweeney had butchered those transients discovered in Stowe Township! On the other hand, what if Merylo were right? Perhaps the Frank Sweeney that he and Zalewski interrogated on February 5, 1940—

the man Merylo described as "delicate" and "fat and soft" — really was incapable of committing the boxcar butcheries. Could there, indeed, be a second killer out there, one with an MO somewhat similar to the Butcher's? There seemed no way to know for sure, but David Cowles and Eliot Ness owed it to Cleveland and to the law enforcement officials from neighboring cities in Ohio and Pennsylvania — municipalities that had been swept up in the ongoing torrent of horror — to explore every possibility. The city of Cleveland, therefore, went to the considerable trouble and expense of having the remains of the three boxcar victims brought to the Western Reserve Medical School by a licensed city undertaker for further examination. Moreover, in July 1940 — a mere two months after the terrible discovery in Stowe Township — Merylo was granted permission to go undercover, to ride the rails like a bum, in a desperate search for clues as to the Butcher's identity — perhaps to reveal him as Frank Sweeney, perhaps, as someone else.

At this point, a black hole opens in the investigative trail: once the boxcar victims' remains had been delivered to the precincts of the medical school, the flow of information surrounding them simply stopped cold. No single document of any kind has survived. In fact, not even a lingering rumor remains as to what conclusions pathologists arrived at after studying those remains and comparing those results to the results from the Cleveland victims. Likewise, no record survives of the official reaction of Merylo's superiors to the disappointingly meager results of his three-week journey with Frank Vorell into the hobo twilight world. All that has survived is the negative evidence of Cleveland's disinterest in further developments in Pennsylvania. Official Cleveland just did not care anymore; the heavy weight of informed opinion in the city clearly had dismissed the possibility of any connection between the killings in Cleveland and Pennsylvania. When David Cowles discussed the torso murders in his 1983 taped interview, he never mentioned Pennsylvania; his entire focus remained on Cleveland and the machinations behind the secret interrogation of Frank Sweeney, a man he identified as their only serious suspect. Only a precious few post-investigation comments about the murders from those who participated directly have survived, and none of them — with the sole exception of Peter Merylo's, of course — even hint at a Cleveland-Pennsylvania link.

A FINAL RECKONING

Were all twenty-nine of the murder-dismemberments in Cleveland and Pennsylvania between the years 1921 and 1950 the work of the same individual? Most assuredly not. In order to believe that, one would have to grant the killer an exceedingly long and incredibly convoluted criminal career with a great many stops and starts, constant morphing between organized and disorganized crime scenes, inexplicable changes in victimology and disposal sites he used, abrupt switches in his choice of weapons, and variations in his skill in dismembering his victims. It simply defies all logic that a single person would begin his reign of terror in 1921 with the sexual assault and murder of an elderly woman in her home, suddenly switch to killing and dismembering children, jump to populating an impenetrable Pennsylvania swamp with carefully hidden victims that bore evidence of mob murder, get antsy and move to Cleveland, where instead of hiding his work he displays or carelessly scatters it, scurry off first to Youngstown and then back to Pennsylvania, where he suddenly decides railroad cars are his ideal dump sites, and finally end his career by returning to Cleveland in 1950 for one last hurrah around a pile of steel girders near the downtown area.

How many perpetrators were operating during the thirty-year series of murder-dismemberments in two states popularly referred to as the Torso Murders? We will probably never know with complete certainty. Too much evidence has been lost, and some of what remains is inconclusive. Despite such doubts and uncertainties, however, it seems probable that the fourteen Cleveland victims were dispatched by the same individual, most likely Dr. Francis Edward Sweeney, the only man ever to be seriously considered by Eliot Ness's office. Sweeney could not be responsible for the Murder Swamp killings, however. There is absolutely no evidence that he ever visited New Castle, and even if he had, he could not have become sufficiently familiar with Murder Swamp's myriad hidden, twisting paths to hide so many bodies there. More to the point, during that period, in the mid-1920s, he was attending classes at the University of St. Louis Medical School. It defies all logic that he, or anyone in similar circumstances, would sneak off to an out-of-the-way city several states away for the sole purpose of picking up and murdering total strangers. When Peter Merylo and Martin Zalewski interviewed Sweeney on February 5, 1940, Merylo concluded that he could not have been responsible for any of the murders, primarily because he was too "fat" and "soft" to ride the rails. (It should be remembered at the time of this interrogation, the triple discovery in Stowe Township was three months away.) Merylo was undoubtedly right; the man he saw that day in February 1940 would have been physically incapable of moving through the dark world of lonely railroad lines and deserted boxcars, committing violent murder and terrible mutilation. Sweeney's surviving medical records from the same period also describe him as obese, thus confirming Merylo's observation. But was he always so heavy? When he graduated from Western Reserve University with a pharmacology degree in 1923, his yearbook picture shows a man with a long, lean face. Subsequent photographs from his years in St. Louis (1925–29) reveal a somewhat fuller face, but he still does not appear obese. At what point in his life did his weight become incapacitation? We are unlikely ever to be able to determine his physical condition in the mid-1930s, when the Cleveland murders began, but there is no reason to assume he was as heavy and potentially incapacitated then as he was to become five years later.

As nearly as can be determined from the admittedly fragmentary evidence that survives, Peter Merylo seems to be the only law enforcement officer from Cleveland who believed firmly that all the murders he knew of in both states were the work of the same killer. John Flynn was doubtful about a Cleveland-Pennsylvania link after checking into the Murder Swamp victims from the 1920s; David Cowles cautiously hinted at a possible connection in the late 1930s and early 1940s during the investigation into the boxcar victims, but he always remained dubious. Even if we eliminate the bodies discovered in New Castle's Murder Swamp in the mid-1920s as the work of bootleggers or other nefarious characters bent on hiding a body for their own reasons, that still leaves the cluster of dismembered corpses found in railroad cars in 1939 and 1940. Even if we eliminate Francis Sweeney for those grisly deaths, in part because his poor physical condition would have rendered him incapable of riding the rails, it seems clear from the similarity of the MOs that the same killer (or killers working together) bore responsibility for that particular cluster of deaths. The evidence indicates that the killer (or killers) knew the layout of the land, was familiar with the intricacies of the railroad lines between Youngstown and Pittsburgh, and was fully aware of the movements and ultimate fates of old boxcars.

At the time of the murders and for years afterward, Youngstown, Ohio, had the unenviable reputation of being a mob town. It is not out of the question to suggest that the four railroad-related murders of 1939 and 1940 (those of the young man whose body was found in Murder Swamp and whose head was found in a railroad gondola car in October 1939 and the three people found in boxcars on May 3, 1940) may have been the work of local mobsters, though it is difficult to understand what a down-and-out derelict such as James Nicholson could have possibly done to earn the unwanted attention of mob hit men.

I seriously doubt whether it will ever be possible to know exactly how many killers were operating during that crucial thirty-year period. The breakdown that follows results from a consideration of the surviving documents, common sense, logic, intuition (deriving from having lived intimately with the torso murders for more than twenty years), and simple guesswork.

1. 1921: Emma Jackson murdered in Wampum, Pennsylvania by a person unknown—perhaps, the black man who came to the door the day before her death. A wholly isolated event.
2. 1923–25: Two young children—one identified as Luigi Noschesi—murdered, dismembered, and decapitated by an unknown killer, one south of Wampum, the other west of Elwood City, Pennsylvania. Given the ages of the victims, the proximity of both the time of the killings, and the geographical area in which the torsos were found, plus the manner of mutilation, it is likely that a single perpetrator killed both, but that person was not responsible for any of the other deaths.
3. 1923–24: The murders of Charles McGregor and an unidentified male, pieces of whom were found in a freight car of cinders in Weirton, West Virginia. The two men may have been dispatched and mutilated by the same perpetrator, but that individual was not responsible for the other murders from the early 1920s, the Murder Swamp killings, the Cleveland torso murders, or the boxcar butcheries of May 1940.
4. 1925–40: The six victims found in New Castle's Murder Swamp. There is no way to tell how many perpetrators there may have been, but it seems likely that all these deaths were related to the area's bootlegging wars or other mob activity. In every case, there was an obvious attempt to hide the body and a concerted effort to prevent

identification. The perpetrator or perpetrators of these murders were not, however, responsible for the murders in Cleveland or the railroad car killings.

5. 1934–50: The twelve officially recognized victims of Cleveland's Mad Butcher of Kingsbury Run, plus the Lady of the Lake (1934) and Robert Robertson (1950). Francis Edward Sweeney, the deranged doctor who was Eliot Ness's prime suspect, remains the most likely perpetrator.

6. 1936–40: The four victims found in railroad cars. The MOs used in these killings and the disposal of the victims' bodies are closest to those employed by the Butcher in Cleveland, but there are significant differences. Most likely all four boxcar victims were killed by a single perpetrator, but he was not responsible for either the earlier Murder Swamp killings or the Cleveland butcheries.

Since 1992, Robert Mancini, a resident of Austintown, Ohio, has worked on the theory that Peter Merylo was correct in his judgment that a single murderer killed all the victims in Cleveland and Pennsylvania and that this killer was, indeed, a railroad man, most likely based in New Castle. After years of digging through New Castle railroad records in search of a likely candidate, Mancini ultimately settled on Thomas Hunter Perrill, a one-time brakeman, switchman, and conductor, as the notorious Butcher. Born in West Virginia in 1899, Perrill worked on the railroads before eventually enlisting in the army in 1942, at the age of forty-three, only to meet a suspicious death by fire in a latrine accident—an explosion of some sort—on a Louisiana military base. The biggest problem with Mancini's candidate for the Butcher's mantle is Perrill's small stature; at a mere five feet six inches tall and weighing a meager 148 pounds, Perrill would have been too small to overpower the Butcher's more husky victims and completely incapable of carrying their corpses over the rugged terrain of Kingsbury Run. The same objection does not apply to the railroad car victims found in Pennsylvania, however, since the three boxcar victims of May 3, 1940, were likewise of slight build. Perrill may not have been the Mad Butcher of Kingsbury Run, but is it conceivable that he was the Boxcar Butcher of Stowe Township? This theory is attractive, but is most likely incorrect; the large bloody footprint found in one of the boxcars would argue against such a conclusion.

APOCRYPHA

In the years since Cleveland's most notorious murders rocked the city, a cottage industry has sprung up devoted to giving the Mad Butcher ever more victims in an ever-expanding geographic area of activity. Regrettably, Peter Merylo must take responsibility for getting the whole process started in the late 1930s. He never wavered in his belief that a single murderer was responsible both for Cleveland's torso murders and for many of those in Pennsylvania, and an eager local press willingly gave him a pulpit for preaching his opinions. Confusion in the numbering of victims outside Ohio began literally with the first visit by Cleveland officials to New Castle in 1937. What follows is a consideration of other murder-dismemberment victims whose deaths have been attributed, at one time or another, to Cleveland's Mad Butcher. It should be pointed out that Merylo did not believe all the murders in Pennsylvania were the work of the Butcher and even initially considered some to be legitimate victims, only to reject them later.

ADDITIONAL MURDERS ATTRIBUTED TO THE CLEVELAND BUTCHER: 1941–1947

May 26–31, 1941
The discovery of two amputated male legs in the Ohio River. No other body parts found; victim never identified.

Hopping off a freight train at Aliquippa, Pennsylvania, Albert H. Smoot and John Omuska were almost immediately confronted by an amputated male leg on a bank of the Ohio River near the Sewickley Bridge and the P&LE Railroad. Allegheny County detectives Sam Grahm and Lester Leonard, the first law men on the scene, examined the cleanly severed limb and immediately dismissed the notion that the dismemberment could have been caused by the paddlewheel of a passing steamboat. As they stared at the gruesome find, the minds of both men wandered back to May 3, 1940, and the horrible discoveries made in a string of boxcars in Stowe Township. Had the Mad Butcher of Kingsbury Run struck again?

Five days later, two nineteen-year-old men—William Kraus and Eugene Lewicki—were rowing in a back channel of the Ohio River near Coraopolis, Pennsylvania, when they came upon a second male leg; authorities surmised that it probably came from the same body as the first one found. Again, investigators' thoughts immediately turned to the boxcar murders of 1940 and to Cleveland's Mad Butcher. Cleveland police were duly alerted, and on June 1, Peter Merylo and John Sullivan arrived in Pittsburgh to consult with local authorities. Ironically, the pair spoke with Samuel Riddle, the same officer who had reported formally on the Stowe Township discoveries the year before.

The rest of the body was never found, and no official paperwork dealing with these two legs has survived in the files of the Allegheny County coroner's office. The *Pittsburgh Press* mentioned the apparent skill with which the disarticulation had been managed, but this totally uncorroborated speculation is hardly enough to tie them to Cleveland's Mad Butcher.

September 24, 1941
Body of a decapitated white male discovered in a dump near the P&LE Railroad tracks along the Monongahela River. Head found about thirty feet away; victim identified as Wallace L. Brown.

In a scene eerily reminiscent of the discovery in Cleveland of victims 11 and 12 three years before, three men foraging for scrap iron in a Pittsburgh dump found the shoeless, headless corpse of Wallace Brown, covered with wrapping paper and wooden planks. The police immediately dismissed the possibility that Brown had been decapitated by a passing train and pointed to the lack of blood on the site as proof that his murder and beheading had occurred somewhere else, most likely across the river on the Hazelwood side. The thirty-five-year-old victim was a rather unsavory character himself, an ex-convict sporting a rap sheet that extended back to 1933 and included arrests for burglary and larceny. After his release in January from the County Workhouse, where he had been serving a sentence for receiving stolen goods, Brown had been supporting himself by working at a series of odd jobs (although the Coroner's Jury Verdict listed his profession as janitor) and had last been seen two or three days before his death by Grace Neuman, a woman for whom he had been working. She had summarily ordered him off her property when he had showed up drunk and suddenly turned abusive.

Pittsburgh police also dismissed the notion that Brown had been a victim of the Mad Butcher and apparently made no attempt to alert Cleveland authorities to the grim discovery. None of Peter Merylo's surviving police reports deal directly with Brown, nor is he mentioned in the detective's memoirs. The sole reference to Wallace Brown in any of Merylo's papers occurs in a letter of July 31, 1944 (see the passage excerpted below). The autopsy protocol notes a number of "irregular serrated and tooth-like cuts" in the skin at the points of decapitation, suggesting that Brown had been decapitated with a saw rather than a large knife, the Mad Butcher's instrument of choice. The coroner also noted bruise-like discoloration and a number of small abrasions on the forehead but stopped short of suggesting these were signs of an attack.

June 21, 1942
Body of a decapitated white male discovered in the Monongahela River near Pittsburgh. Head never recovered; victim later identified as Ernest Alonzo.

It was on a Sunday afternoon that two members of the Coast Guards, Glenwood DeJardine and D. L. Cave, came across the nude, headless body of a white male floating in the Monongahela at the upper end of Lock No. 1 near the 10th Street Bridge while on routine river patrol duty. Since the body was later judged to have been in the water for between twelve and eighteen hours, the only possibilities for identification rested with fingerprints, a couple of vaccination marks on the left arm, and an old surgical scar on the abdomen. The next day, fingerprint records from Harrisburg positively identified the victim as Ernest Alonzo, a thirty-three-year-old unemployed Mexican immigrant from Donora, Pennsylvania, with a record of heavy drinking and barroom brawls. Alonzo had last been seen alive in a decidedly inebriated condition by his father on Friday, June 19. Disgusted and frustrated by his son's persistent alcohol problems, the elder Alonzo had chastised Ernest for his drunkenness and ordered him home to sleep it off. Sometime very late Friday or early Saturday, Alonzo met the man who would murder him, cut off his head (which was never recovered), and toss his body into the Monongahela River.

The autopsy was performed by Coroner Theodore R. Helmbold, the same man who had handled the formal procedures of the three butchered men found in derelict boxcars on May 3, 1940. "The head had been removed at approximately the level of the junction of the neck and shoulders," he wrote in the formal protocol. "The skin had been cut through by a series of incisions varying from 3 to 4 inches in length and these were over-lapping so that tag-like pieces of skin occurred where one incision ended and the other started."

Despite some speculation in the press, no one in Pittsburgh's official circles thought there was any link between the Alonzo killing and the Kingsbury Run murders; and one need only read the full coverage in local newspapers to understand why. "Unlike the workman like technique of the 'Mad Butcher of Kingsbury Run,'" wrote the *Pittsburgh Press* on Monday, June 22, "the man's neck had been hacked several times before the bones were severed." Alonzo's throat had, indeed, been slashed with a knife, but his head had been chopped off by multiple blows from a meat cleaver or an axe. No one in Pennsylvania even bothered to alert Cleveland police to the Alonzo murder. In an official report dated August 17, Merylo wrote to his superior, Lieutenant George Smyth, "I also wish to advise Inspector [Walter C.] Monaghan [of the Pittsburgh Police Department] that this department did not receive any information on the headless body found in the Mononghallia [sic] River in Pittsburgh, Pa. about 2 months ago and if it is possible, we would apprecite [sic] if he would send us a copy of same." The next day, Chief Matowitz dutifully made the formal request, but Pittsburgh police did not respond until August 28. No one in Cleveland officialdom showed any interest in the document; the only surviving copy of the autopsy protocol sent to Cleveland is in

Peter Merylo's files. Whoever murdered Ernest Alonzo, hacked off his head, and dumped his corpse into the Monongahela did so either in a blind rage or from implacable hatred—perhaps both—but that killer, who was never identified, was not the Mad Butcher of Kingsbury Run.

—

As nearly as I can determine, no one in Pittsburgh law enforcement ever suggested that Ernest Alonzo and Wallace Brown may have been victims of the same killer, but that would seem to be a distinct possibility. Both men were in their mid-thirties, either out of work or minimally employed; both had been seen drunk before death; and both were found in or close to the Monongahela River, approximately three miles apart. It may be the sheerest of coincidences, but James Nicholson—the third of the three victims found on May 3, 1940—was of a similar age and background. (Since the other two men found on that May morning were never identified, it's impossible to say if they also fit a similar profile.) On July 31, 1944, Peter Merylo, now in retirement from the Cleveland Police Department, wrote a letter to Lieutenant Martin J. Crowley of the Pennsylvania State Police advising him that he had interviewed a man institutionalized in the Athens (Ohio) State Hospital, Andrew Longa, and had concluded that Longa could not be the Mad Butcher of Kingsbury Run. (Merylo's letter is obviously a reply to a formal request of some sort, now unfortunately lost.) He closes this bit of semiofficial correspondence with a rather interesting statement. "I am of the opinion," wrote Merylo, "that the same man is responsible for [Ernest] Alonzo's death, who dissected another man whose legs were found in the Ohio River at Stowe Township and Seweckly [*sic*] on May 31, 1941 and another decapitated body that was found in 1940, in the city dump of Pittsburgh, located along the Monongahela River. This body was identified through finger prints as Wallace Lloyd Brown."

This quotation clearly indicates that in 1944 Merylo was including these three men in his tally of Mad Butcher victims, despite the fact that the coroner's reports for Alonzo and Brown did not support such an assumption. By 1952, when Paul McClung's article covering the case appeared in *Front Page Detective*, Merylo appears to have backed away from that judgment, for neither man is mentioned by name. At least part of Merylo's conclusion about this particular cluster of victims may have been correct, however. While the evidence does not support their having been killed by Cleveland's Butcher, it does support the possibility—even the probability—that Alonzo, Brown, and the unidentified owner of the two legs found in the Ohio River were the victims of a single perpetrator. The similarities in the ages and habits of Alonzo and Brown, the proximity of the dump sites for all three victims, and the relatively brief time span (just over a year) in which the murders occurred support such a possibility. The descriptions in Alonzo's and Brown's autopsy protocols of their sloppy decapitations, however, make it clear that this unidentified killer was not the Mad Butcher of Kingsbury Run.

June 28, 1942
Disarticulated remains of a decapitated African American prostitute discovered under the Sidway Bridge in Kingsbury Run. Victim later identified as nineteen-year-old Margaret (Marie) Francis Wilson,

While playing in the Run, three young African American boys made the gruesome discovery of Margaret Wilson's remains that would turn into one of the most bizarre episodes of the torso murder saga. A man identified as Willie Johnson had been observed getting out of a cab and depositing a trunk containing Wilson's remains under the bridge. Arrested, tried, convicted, and executed for Wilson's murder, Johnson offered the most ludicrous explanation imaginable to explain his actions, claiming that he had knocked Wilson out during an argument with her and then simply gone to bed, only to awaken sometime later to find her body inexplicably cut up in pieces all over the floor. In spite of a brief and misguided flurry of guessing in the local press, neither the Wilson killing nor Willie Johnson himself was ever linked to the earlier murders in Kingsbury Run; her body had been disarticulated with a saw, not a large knife. Willie Johnson was not the Mad Butcher of Kingsbury Run.

July 1945
The nude, decapitated, and disarticulated bodies of two men found in a gunny sack on the banks of the Hudson River in New York City. Heads never recovered; one victim later identified.

There is almost no extant information on these particular murders other than the fact that one of the victims was identified as a low-level New Jersey hood with a record of sexual deviance; no record of the name of this hood has survived. It isn't even clear whether the remains of both men had been stuffed into a single sack or two separate bags. Since Merylo had retired from the police force two years before these remains turned up, he did not follow up on this discovery or leave any sort of official report. It is highly unlikely that these two men were victims of the Mad Butcher, and there is little evidence that even Peter Merylo thought they were. He does not mention these murder victims in either set of his memoirs. (In fairness, I should point out that Merylo may have dictated the memoirs before these remains were found in July 1945.) In his 1949 article in *Harper's Magazine*, John Bartlow Martin likewise omits any mention of them, although Paul McClung does list them among the Butcher's targets in his July 1952 article in *Front Page Detective*. There were never any other murders in the New York area at the time that were attributed to the Cleveland Butcher. It is also highly unlikely that the Butcher would desert the Ohio-Pennsylvania area for a brief stopover in New York State, where he just happened to link up with a know pervert and hood. Given the nature of the identified victim, it is far more likely that both men were casualties of local underworld activity. Without a specific date or a name for the identified victim, however, it is impossible to track down the autopsy protocols in the New York coroner's office.

January 15, 1947
The murder of Elizabeth Short, also known as the Black Dahlia, in Los Angeles, California. Victim not decapitated, but her body bisected and mutilated.

I include this infamous, exceptionally gruesome, and officially unsolved murder in a listing of the Cleveland Butcher's possible victims only because more than two decades of pop culture insist on putting her there. The seeds of popular belief in a link between her murder and the Cleveland torso murders were probably sown as far back as late December 1938, when Cleveland's police chief, Matowitz, received a very strange anonymous letter.

> You can rest easy now, as I have come out to sunny California for the winter. I felt bad operating on those people, but science must advance. I shall astonde [*sic*] the medical profession, a man with only a D. C. [doctor of chiropractic medicine].

What did their lives mean in comparison to hundreds of sick and disease-twisted bodies? Just laboratory guinea pigs found on any public street. No one missed them when I failed. My last case was successful. I now know the feeling of Pasteur, Thoreau and other pioneers.

Right now I have a volunteer who will absolutely prove my theory. They call me mad and a butcherer, but the truth will out.

I have failed but once here. The body has not been found and never will be, but the head minus the features is buried on Century Boulevard, between Western and Crenshaw. I feel it is my duty to dispose of the bodies as I do. It is God's will not to let them suffer.

X

Predictably, this curious missive received full play in the Cleveland press, and Merylo initially deemed it one of the best leads in the torso case up to that point. Los Angeles police were, of course, informed, but when they dutifully explored the spot the writer had designated, they found nothing. Within a year, Merylo had changed his mind about the odd bit of correspondence for some unspecified reason, dismissing it as the ravings of a crank. In 1942, authorities in California zeroed in on Charles August DiVere, a seemingly deranged quack physician, as the likely source of the letter, although no one ever tied him to Cleveland or, for that matter, to western Pennsylvania. This lack of any corroborating evidence did not seem to matter; the theory of a link between Cleveland and Los Angeles entered true crime folklore.

At this point, the supposed connection was nothing more than an interesting footnote, but the theory received a decided boost in the late 1980s, when NBC's *Unsolved Mysteries*—hosted by Robert Stack—presented a segment, in the show's typical pseudo-documentary style, alleging that Cleveland's Mad Butcher had, indeed, packed up his knife and headed for a life of murder and dismemberment in the California sunshine, where he, in due course, committed one of the most heinous murders in American history—that of Elizabeth Short. Perhaps, the most glaring inaccuracy in the entire presentation was the depiction of the Mad Butcher as a wimpy little man who looked as if he would be more comfortable as the day-dreaming protagonist of a James Thurber story than as a knife-wielding phantom menace stalking the desolation of Kingsbury Run, the impenetrable tangle of Murder Swamp, or the bleak landscapes of the Depression-era railroad lines. At the time of the murders, virtually every portrait fashioned of the killer in both Cleveland and Pennsylvania pictured him as a large, powerful man—not a weak little accountant.

For many Americans, however, television speaks a greater truth than any other medium or the most respected public figure; this single episode of *Unsolved Mysteries* so firmly established the notion of a link between the Kingsbury Run and the Black Dahlia slayings, that in the early 1990s, the Los Angeles Police Department contacted its Cleveland counterpart with a request to investigate the possibility of a connection between the two cold cases. In response, Edward Kovacic, who was then Cleveland's chief of police, turned over this undeniably intriguing investigative plumb to John Fransen of the homicide unit. Although he delved deeply into Cleveland's most famous lurid horrors, Fransen (now retired) quickly dismissed the notion that the Kingsbury Run Butcher had anything to do with the horrible death of the Black Dahlia. Beyond the facts that her body was bisected and put on display for maximum shock value, nothing about Elizabeth Short's murder remotely resembled the work of Cleveland's Butcher. The severe lacerations on her face, the mutilations made to other parts of her body, and the fact she was obviously tortured, simply were not part of the Butcher's MO. Also, in spite of all the grotesque indignities her killer inflicted on her body, Elizabeth Short had not been beheaded, and decapitation, more than anything else, defined the Butcher's style.

John Gilmore's *Severed* remains the only reliable treatment of the Black Dahlia case. In his detailed exploration of Elizabeth Short's shocking murder, Gilmore focuses on Jack Anderson Wilson as her murderer. Standing well over six feet tall, Wilson (also known as Glover Loving and Arnold Smith) was a gaunt, cross-dressing alcoholic hobbled by a pronounced limp. He had an impressively long criminal record and obviously knew something about the Dahlia killing; he even seemed inclined to share his long-harbored secrets, but strictly on his own terms. Over a period of months, Gilmore persuaded the elusive Wilson to meet him several times in a seedy bar, an erratic and maddening collection of encounters during which the perpetually evasive Wilson drank and rambled on endlessly. Often accompanying his disjointed discourse with a show-and-tell of Elizabeth Short memorabilia, including a photograph he would not allow Gilmore to touch, Wilson occasionally punctuated his chain of cryptic pronouncements with stark revelations about the Dahlia murder that only someone directly involved would be able to make. Gilmore ultimately came to regard Wilson not only as the most viable suspect in Elizabeth Short's murder but also as the most likely candidate for another Los Angeles killing, that of twenty-year-old socialite Georgette Bauerdorf on October 12, 1944. Before anyone in law enforcement could officially move on Wilson, however, the enigmatic down-and-outer burned to death in his flea-bag hotel room, along with his priceless collection of Elizabeth Short artifacts.

For those convinced of a link between the murder-mutilation of Elizabeth Short and the butcheries in Cleveland and western Pennsylvania, if Jack Anderson Wilson now topped the list of viable suspects in the former, he must be guilty of, the latter as well. It is easy to place him in the region of northeastern Ohio in the mid-1930s; Wilson had been born south of Cleveland in Canton, Ohio. At that time, though, he was barely into his teens, and it strains credulity to believe that anyone so young could travel alone to Cleveland, establish some sort of relationship with the much older people who would become the Butcher's victims, and overpower them—especially someone like Edward Andrassy—Cleveland's victim 1—who was rumored to carry an ice pick. It also seems highly unlikely that a teen could move easily through the ugly landscape of cheap bars and shanty towns where the Butcher apparently trolled for his victims without attracting attention, and while the surviving police reports record a plethora of oddballs as potential suspects, they make no mention of a suspicious, alarmingly tall teenager. Since 2011, John Gilmore and I have traded e-mails dealing with Wilson and his possible connection to the torso murders, a link he has always rejected. "Jack Anderson Wilson had nothing to do with the Mad Butcher," he bluntly maintained in an e-mail of March 8, 2011, "other than to show interest, if not fascination, in the case and the display of one of the victim's heads (a model thereof). [A casting of the head of victim 4 was displayed at the Great Lakes Exposition in the summers of 1936 and 1937 in hopes that someone might recognize him.] Wilson would have been far too young to have been engaged in beheadings of adults. Linking Wilson with the Butcher has been a repeated attempt over thirty years or so that I know of, and it just ain't so."

—

The savage echoes from those three decades of mayhem still reverber-
ate in the atmosphere of eastern Ohio and western Pennsylvania, and
in the minds of their residents. Spurred by the sheer ghastliness of
the events and the fact that no perpetrator or perpetrators were ever
definitively identified, the murder-dismemberments of Cleveland's
Kingsbury Run, New Castle's Murder Swamp, and the railroad lines
linking the two desolate spots have grown into a true crime legend.
Like all legends, the saga of the torso murders ultimately evolved into
a bewildering, cloudy combination of fact and fiction. Local television
stations, newspapers, and magazines still occasionally respond to the
distant howls of those terrible crimes with stories of one sort or another:
an anniversary piece, a literary treatment of one or more of the cases,
or a retrospective prompted by any killing or series of killings remotely
similar to the torso murders. When the city of Cleveland learned of
Anthony Sowell, a serial killer who had secreted the bodies of eleven
women in his house and backyard, the specters of Kingsbury Run
silently raised their heads, prompting local television stations to call
me asking for comments on the supposed similarities between Sowell
and the Mad Butcher of Kingsbury Run.

Kingsbury Run is quiet now. Blighted by decay, the neighborhoods
on either side of the gorge have retreated from its edges. Except for the
periodic rattle of the rapid transits, little breaks the eerie silence except
the forlorn sighs of an occasional factory whistle and the howl of the
wind. The infamous New Castle–West Pittsburg Murder Swamp also
slumbers. The little of it that remains—the vestige not mown down
and covered over with dirt—has been chained off from the surrounding area. The spot where the grimly determined search party gathered
in 1925 is overgrown with weeds. Now old and rusty, the once-busy
railroad lines stretch silently through a crumbling industrial landscape
in both Ohio and Pennsylvania. The thunderous chugging of massive
steam locomotives is little more than a faded memory. Derelict buildings, many close to collapse, dot the borders of the iron pathways.
Everywhere there is utter silence, the ominous silence of a desolate
wasteland where ghosts still hover, guarding their long-buried secrets.

APPENDIX

LUKE G. MOUSSA

The purpose of the following study is to determine how closely the victimology (also known as the victim profile) of the dead discussed in chapter 6, to which I collectively refer as the Murder Swamp series (figure 1), resembles that of the fourteen recognized victims of the Cleveland Butcher, referred to here as the Cleveland Torso series.

The model of analysis that accomplishes this study is a Standardized Point System that retroactively analyzes researched information by tabulating attributes that are specific to the victims of both series of murders, on a singular and collective level, and displaying those findings as descriptive statistics. The analysis will focus on victimology and crime scene characteristics for two main reasons. Firstly, these two aspects of the murders provide a window into an offender's psyche and serve as the building blocks for investigation. Secondly, the only substantiated evidence in the Murder Swamp series are the victimology and crime scene reports; whereas in the Cleveland Torso series other evidence from the investigations is available (for example, rosters of suspect ranking, interrogation dialogues, and detailed post-mortem reports), no such evidence survives (if it ever existed) from the investigations into the Murder Swamp series. Because of the disparity in the amount of detailed information available from the two series, correlations—here termed *linkages*—will be used to better understand the relationship between the events occurring in Pennsylvania and those occurring in Ohio.

It is pertinent that the reader understands the bias that may arise by studying only the victimology in a series. A good example of this problem may be found in the murder series perpetrated by Nathaniel Code in the

Victims		Date of Discovery
Victim 01	Emma Jackson	3/16/1921
Victim 02	Jane Doe 1	7/11/1923
Victim 03	Charles "Chuck" McGregor	10/1/1923
Victim 04	John Doe 1	2/11/1924
Victim 05	Luigi Noschesi	1/1/1925
Victim 06	John Doe 2 "Unknown Man"	10/6/1925
Victim 07	John Doe 3	10/17/1925
Victim 08	Jane Doe 2	10/19/1925
Victim 09	John Doe 4	10/15/1934
Victim 10	John Doe 5	7/1/1936
Victim 11	John Doe 6	10/8/1939
Victim 12	John Doe 7	5/3/1940
Victim 13	John Doe 8	5/3/1940
Victim 14	James David Nicholson	5/3/1940
Victim 15	John Doe 9	11/2/1940

Figure 1. Victim Date of Discovery

1980s. Code's victims included men, women, and children of different ages. Since he also used a variety of methods to dispatch his victims, no clear linkage would have emerged if one had studied only the victim profile. However, by also studying other attributes of the crime, investigators were able to identify constant variables, such as Code's positioning of all his victims facedown and his use of electric or telephone cord, tied in a unique fashion, to bind them.

The murders perpetrated by a killer by the name of Morris Frampton in 1977 provide another example of the bias created by studying victimology alone. Since Frampton was racially indiscriminant in his choice of victims, a study of victim profiles only would not have revealed the linkages in Frampton's series of murders. Instead of focusing on the variations in modes of operation (MOs) and victim profiles, therefore, we look at what was present at the crime scenes—the psychological stamp the killer left behind. In the Frampton series, investigators uncovered the linkages among the murders by observing the ritualistic behavior that spanned the crime scenes. Frampton's psychological stamp was overkill, including extreme blunt trauma to the heads and trunks of his victims. In this series, death was a symptom of the tremendous beatings suffered. It became apparent that all this killer required was for his victims to be female, and, for the killer, in the right place at the right time—that is, in a place and time that gave Frampton the opportunity to commit the crime and get away with it. Frampton understood that by trolling for prostitutes, his risk/cost ratio was low and his reward was high. Therefore, in the offender's rationale, this type of "high-risk" victim met his typology, but the race or age of the victim was irrelevant. Another murderer, Albert DeSalvo, once commented that it didn't matter what kind of woman he raped and killed, stating, "It really was Woman that I wanted—not any special one, just Woman with what a woman has" (Lester 1995, 19).

It is obvious that inaccuracies can arise when investigators study only the victimology in a series of crimes, as opposed to studying it in conjunction with the other elements that they have uncovered. The study of victimology is only one of the techniques that law officers use in investigations. Nevertheless, this study focuses on victimology in a pragmatic and intuitive manner. Essentially we are connecting the dots to construct a picture. This study does not attempt to speculate about the number or identity of the offenders involved, but instead uses facts on record, drawn from the victimology, postmortem, and crime scene reports that still exist. This model in no way attempts to address the psychology of the offender or offenders in either series of murders. (The psychology of the perpetrator of the Cleveland Torso series was evaluated in depth by Dr. Cathleen Cerny [in Badal 2010, 180–92]). For visual representation, geographic maps contained within this appendix give the approximated locations of the discovery sites of the victims. The coordinates displayed on the maps are based on the descriptions drawn from the research and documents available.

Throughout this process, the logic and methodology will be clearly outlined in order to produce a transparent paradigm. Since this study is not intended for statisticians, it will not include equations; those interested in the calculations will find them summarized in the narrative. The analysis continually asks questions in order to gain insight. At times, such a question simply cannot be answered, and we are left with the unknown. When these instances of uncertainty arise during the phases of analysis, they are given the designation *null.* This data of unknown answers is factored into the model throughout the processes, thus maintaining the model's empirical and standardized approach. Although a geographic profile was performed in a prior study of the Cleveland Torso series, the Murder Swamp series lacks the information essential for generating a substantiated profile. Because of this, we will touch only lightly on some concepts of spatial statistics and geographic profiling when the need arises.[1]

To summarize, we are disassembling what is known in order view the specifics of each crime. The data is then organized and reassembled into a database so that it can be queried to give the results essential in determining the final output of the model. This analysis is divided into four parts: the acquisition and organization of data as it pertains to the victims; the identification and evaluation of said data; the standardization and disqualification of data; and, finally, the presentation of findings, and concluding arguments.

DATA SUMMARY

Software programs used in this analysis include Environmental Systems Research Institute's ArcInfo 10, Google Earth Pro, and Microsoft's Access and Excel. Data pertinent to this study was culled from the information researched by James Jessen Badal.

The study obviously begins with the attainment of data, which are then arranged in order to derive crucial information to answer proposed questions. The victim base analyzed is comprised of the fifteen individuals outlined in chapter 6 that are considered those most closely aligned with both the Cleveland Torso and Murder Swamp series of murders. It should be noted that data pertaining to the Cleveland Torso series was extracted from the research of James Jessen Badal (2001) and Mark Wade Stone (2006).

TERMINOLOGY

Let's take a moment to define the terminology used in the analysis and what each term represents:

Attributes: the details evaluated for each victim in order to designate an event.

Event: a binary number assigned to each attribute which is unique to each of the fifteen victims analyzed. The binary system indicates whether the attribute was present, absent or null.

Null: attributes in which a present or absent event cannot be confirmed are designated as null. Null data is just as critical to the analysis as present or absent events are.

Correlation Linkage: the value assigned to attributes that share similar events among the victims. The value is given a ranking that assigns significance to said attributes, allowing for creation of a database that can be appropriately queried in a guided manner by assigning "weights" to particular attributes. It should be noted that significance does not pertain to probability but only serves as an identifier of the most predominant attributes.

Filters: the combination of attributes that result from the query which produce a phenomenon.

Phenomenon: specific combination of attributes and events that identify the victims who are associated with the filters.

Tiers: ranked from liberal to conservative; there are twenty-six tiers in total, of which thirteen are nonrandom phenomenon and thirteen are random. (Further examination of tiers will follow.)

Liberal and **Conservative:**

> *Liberal:* indicates that results of the phenomenon are more inclusive and the parameters are less restrictive.

> *Conservative:* indicates that results of the phenomenon are more restrictive, leading to more exclusive results; the converse of liberal.

Output: victims identified by observing the phenomenon produced by the filter combination.

ATTRIBUTES AND EVENTS

The first step is to build a database that stores the attributes associated with each victim that indicate whether an event was present, absent, or null. Because little is known about the Murder Swamp victims (for example, residence, family, occupation, or spatial patterns prior to their discovery), the categories decided on are solely related to the victims and what law enforcement personnel witnessed at the crime scenes.

Attributes for this analysis were qualified based on standard observations used in serial crime investigation, then finalized to the attributes reported in the Murder Swamp and Cleveland Torso series. Because we are looking at data in an effort to find correlation linkages between victims and crime scenes, we must first identify what attributes are evaluated, why particular attributes were chosen, and how they factor into the findings. Attributes can be thought of as the specific details witnessed from studying the victim profile and crime scene reports from both murder series. Each attribute field questions whether it (the attribute) was present, absent, or null in relation to the particular victim/crime being evaluated. If the question pertaining to the attribute can be answered, it is recorded as an event. In analyzing victim 1 (Emma Jackson), for example, we might ask if the attribute mutilation was present. Since mutilation (the attribute) was not inflicted upon the victim, we would answer "no" (the binary event). We would then repeat this process with the other attributes, sequentially addressing each attribute and entering an event for each victim. If an attribute was present, we would enter the numeral "1" to indicate its presence; if it were absent, we would enter the numeral "0"; and if we lacked the evidence to ascertain if it was present or absent, we would enter "null."

At this stage we are not analyzing data, but organizing in order to tabulate and understand what attributes are specific to each victim, and which victims share the same attribute/event correlation linkage. The attributes of gender and age each encompass mutually exclusive classifications; the remaining attributes can occur simultaneously. After this tabulation is completed, we continue to the next phase. At this juncture, it is important to explicitly define what was asked of each attribute and how it was qualified. Initially, there were thirteen attributes, shown below in bold. After disqualification, ten remained, shown in bold and underlined.

The first two attributes are divided into mutually exclusive classifications, of which only one event can be entered per classification:

Gender: *Male* or *Female.*
Age:
    Child: less than or equal to age twelve.
    Teen: aged thirteen to nineteen.
    Adult: aged twenty to sixty-five.
    Elder: aged greater than sixty-five.

Although it could be argued that the ages of eighteen and nineteen years should belong to the adult category, I have placed them in the teen category based on semantics; they each have the suffix *teen*. I have also decided against further subdividing each age classification into early and late stages; in a large sample group, this would be the preferred method, but it is unnecessary for the small number of victims studied. Moreover, the majority of victims were adults with an age disparity of about six to seven years between the teen and adult classifications. Lastly, because we are drawing on what we know from the Cleveland Torso series, in conjunction with the Murder Swamp series, it is of value to realize that the youngest victim in the former series was Edward Andrassy, aged twenty-nine.

The evaluation of shared attributes follows the attributes with mutually exclusive characteristics described above. Shared attributes are filtered in two stages. The first stage includes all characteristics witnessed at the crime scenes, as well as the condition of the victim's body. The second stage serves to disqualify certain attributes contingent upon the availability and validity of information. Each attribute is addressed below, and tabulated information on the two stages of filtering can be assessed in figures 2 and 3.

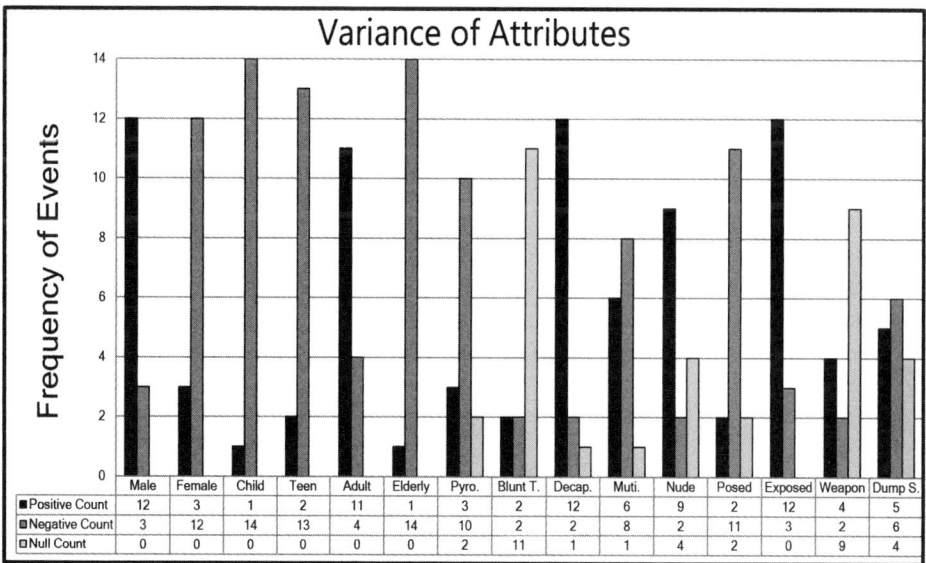

Variance of Attributes

	Male	Female	Child	Teen	Adult	Elderly	Pyro.	Blunt T.	Decap.	Muti.	Nude	Posed	Exposed	Weapon	Dump S.
■ Positive Count	12	3	1	2	11	1	3	2	12	6	9	2	12	4	5
▣ Negative Count	3	12	14	13	4	14	10	2	2	8	2	11	3	2	6
▢ Null Count	0	0	0	0	0	0	2	11	1	1	4	2	0	9	4

Figure 2. Variance of Attributes

Variance of Attributes (revised)

Frequency of Events

	Male	Female	Teen	Adult	Pyro.	Decap.	Muti.	Nude	Posed	Exposed	Dump S.
■Positive Count	12	3	2	11	3	12	6	9	2	12	5
▣Negative Count	3	12	13	4	10	2	8	2	11	3	6
☐Null Count	0	0	0	0	2	1	1	4	2	0	4

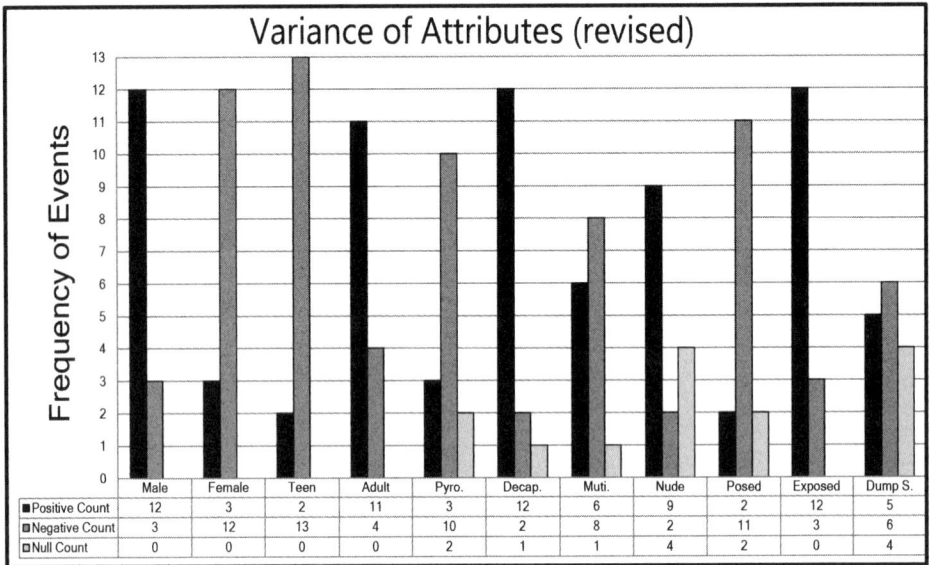

Figure 3. Variance of Attributes (revised)

Pyromania: the evidence of fire. Were burns inflicted upon the body either to dispose of it or to cause pain? The use of fire to dispose of a victim would help to categorize the offender's MO. The use of fire to inflict pain and suffering is not required to successfully commit the crime, so this would be considered ritualistic behavior and might play into the offender's paraphilia. Since the data show few instances of pyromania, it is not considered significant to our study, but it will be retained and used in the filters.

Before moving along, let's take a moment to define the term *signature,* generally understood to mean the combination of the mode of operation and ritualistic behavior over two or more crime scenes. Signature can be used to identify a killer's "calling card"—the habitual repetition of the killer's fantasy that psychologically satisfies his or her needs and is displayed at the crime scene. Richard Keppel defines signature as what the killer "leaves at each crime scene across the spectrum of several murders," and goes on to state that, "the killer's personal expression takes the form of his unique signature, an imprint left by him at the scene, an imprint the killer is psychologically compelled to leave to satisfy himself sexually" (Keppel and Birnes 1997, 2 and 5).

Blunt Trauma: any type of physical abuse inflicted on the victim in order to incapacitate (MO), conversely carried out as part of a sadistic act (ritual).

Decapitation: of the victims in the Murder Swamp series, 80 percent were decapitated. It must be understood that decapitation is the complete and total separation of head from body, not only the separation between cervical vertebrae.

Mutilation: constitutes the complete separation of appendage from body excluding the head, but consisting of the severance of limbs from the trunk or, for example, the removal of a finger, ear, eye, or nose.

Nudity: state and degree of physical exposure of the victim.

Staging: tactic in offender's MO used to derail investigations and conceal the offender's true identity. An example of this attribute was found in the Green River series of murders in Washington State. The killer in this series placed cigarette butts belonging to other people at the victim dump sites. Staging, like ritual, is extremely difficult to detect, even by seasoned law officers. Moreover, staging, like ritual, may not be used by a specific killer at every crime scene. He or she may refrain from staging or ritualistic behavior because of a lack of resources, a lack of time, or an unexpected obstacle. Because there was staging present at crime scenes it was an initial attribute due to its presence. Staging, as defined above, is not underlined and therefore indicated an attribute not included in calculations. As a result, this study does not use staging as one of the final ten attributes.

Posing: a component of ritualistic behavior playing into the fulfillment of the offender's aberrant fantasy. The Boston Strangler, for example, posed his victims with their genitalia facing the door to maximize the horror of those unfortunate enough to discover their bodies.

Exposure: considers the body of the victim as nonsequestered—left without attempt to conceal the crime for an indefinite amount of time.

Weapon Type: whether the sole weapon used was a knife, as opposed to an axe or saw.

Dump Site vs. **Kill Site:** location of a victim at the site where the murder occurred, versus postmortem placement.

Water-bodies: placement of a victim into a river, lake, or reservoir etc.

DATA EVALUATION

The first step is to identify outliers and their associated attributes that would skew data. The next step is to assign unique values and significance to the remaining attributes in order to reassess which attributes should be used in the process. By doing this, we find what is insignificant, unaccounted for, or simply misleading.

Standardized Point System:

The model uses a Standardized Point System, which indicates whether events were present, absent, or null. The overarching goal is to disqualify in order to identify and thus to realize a final output that is conservative. In other words, we are looking to identify those attributes in the Murder Swamp series that are most closely related to those victims in the Cleveland Torso series by taking an objective approach kept in check by the use of standardization and the inclusion of all variables. Again, the purpose is to find similarities between the victims found in the Cleveland Torso series and the victims found in the Murder Swamp series.

The empirical approach adapted to this model takes into account both known and unknown information. By performing this way, we can ensure, as much as possible, empirically based, factual, and unbiased findings. By using what we know and accounting for what we don't know, we can try to form the clearest possible image of events. We are not focused on random pieces of data; it is not the amount of sheer data we look for but the significant pieces crucial to the understanding of the events studied. Imagine being asked to assess several samples of identical jigsaw puzzles at various stages of completion and assigning significance based on the grouping of pieces that give you the most complete picture of the puzzle. You are not interested in how many pieces are involved or sections are completed: one puzzle might have more completed sections than the others but they might only form the border of the puzzle rather than forming more important sections in the center of the picture. Those pieces identified as valuable data are ranked based on each one's contribution to the picture and on how much of the picture each contains individually and then all contain in combination. By combining many attributes (variables) to form a specific phenomenon and asking what the precursors are, we take a retroactive approach to try to make sense of a subject. By allocating attribute *significance,* we can assign a value (ranking) that can be used as a barometer to compare to other findings, thus creating a combination of attributes that will take into account many events, from the victim profile, and produce a specific output; this can be considered a "many-to-many" analytical approach.

Attributes with points scored at .13 (group code 5) are the most significant attributes because they take into account a large percentage of victims and make up a large percentage of attributes when combined and a small percentage when alone (figure 4).

Essentially we are looking for a large value of variables that make up a small percentage of victims. These victims and their attributes are then cross-examined and the count of positive, negative, and null events that take place is recorded. Again, it should be noted that these numbers are arbitrary and statistical significance cannot be implied.

In order to standardize the data observed, and so as not to skew the outcome, the values were then recalculated to exclude these categories. Frequency tables were then regenerated in order to confirm that the numerical values changed proportionately from the first calculation to the second. Using the point system, the positive value was divided by the negative value to give a weight, so that the lower the weight, the higher significance it holds. This means that one particular attribute (independent x variable) accounts for a large percentage of victims (dependent y variables) on its own, but, in combination with other attributes that share the same weight, accounts for a high number of combined attributes

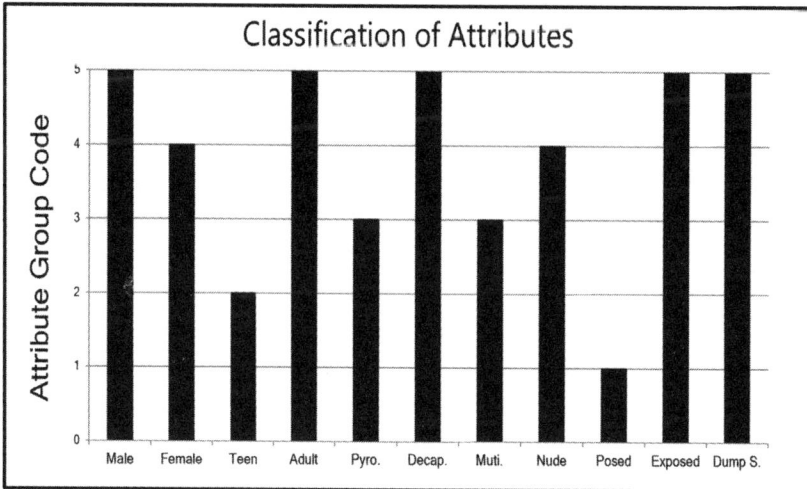

Figure 4. Classification of Attributes

and a low number of victims. Again, the goal is to have many attributes included in the filter combination that in turn yields a low and specific victim output expressed as [$\frac{x2x2}{y\,y}$]. The points were calculated with both the full sample (predisqualification) and the sample with disqualification to confirm again that when variables are removed, their output values change proportionately from the former to the latter.

Although the attributes of blunt trauma and weapon type were declared insufficient to use as a filter based on the above parameters, they are not disregarded because they may provide insight into the final output of victims if they are present. For example, if the filter of adult males who were decapitated and sequestered yields two victims as the output and one indicated a knife was used, we may be able to deduce that a knife was used on the second victim as well if the weapon type field for that victim was null. Attributes with a high weight (e.g., posing) are less significant because they are too specific and return an output that is generated from too narrow a filter. This is expressed as [$\frac{x\,x}{y2y2}$].

We cannot create a conservative filter combination without first observing the results of the liberal. Liberal combinations take into account fewer attribute events and produce a larger output: this is a small/large scenario as represented above. Results that produce a [$\frac{x\,x}{y\,y}$] or [$\frac{x2x2}{y2y2}$], (that is, a 50 percent correlation) are still considered liberal. Only when an attribute outweighs victim results by 51 percent does it enter the conservative realm. This is represented as [$\frac{x2x2}{y\,y}$], or 51/49, or large/small.

Disqualification and Identification:

In order to narrow our attribute fields to the most pertinent information, we will refer to the results of our point system in figure 2. If the sum of null values is larger than the sum of positive and negative values combined, than that particular field must be discounted. In addition, any attribute where only one event is witnessed is rejected, and attributes where there are only two events are not used as filters but are retained to assist in evaluation. The attributes fitting this latter category (that is, that were not used as filters but retained to assist in further evaluation) are teen and posing. The disqualified attributes where the null values exceeded the sum of positive and negative events are blunt trauma and weapon type. Attributes that were disqualified because only one event was observed taking place are child and elderly.

TIER VALUES AND FORMULAS

Tiers were compiled based on significant attributes. Attributes are considered significant based on their event correlation and final score (figure 5).

Values with the lowest score represent a small number of correlated attributes out of the attribute categories. As mentioned before, tiers are ranked from the most liberal to the most conservative based on the classification of attribute to victim ratio. Each tier was randomized using the Excel function *randbetween*. This is used to determine if randomized (actively selected attributes) filter combinations are more significant or just as significant as those built on actively selected attributes. The tier values are the following: *attribute score, value weight, victim score, disparity score, final score, validity, total points,* and *ranking*. Let's take a closer look at these values.

Attribute Score: calculates the percentage of attributes used over the total attributes of the filter. This is calculated by taking the attribute count and dividing it by the total attributes. Specifically, the attribute score constitutes the total count of attributes with a positive event combined to form a filter or search—this is the basis for assigning rank to the tiers.

Value Weight: sums the weight for each attribute's significance score. Each attribute is given a significance score. The lower the score (.13 for this study), the higher the count of events and the lower the null values of this particular attribute, indicating that the attribute is a key piece in assembling and understanding what transpired. Another way to look at score is that while individually an attribute may represent a large number of total victims in the series, as *significant* attributes are identified and then combined, they create a specific and targeted victim output. The attribute score is therefore translated as the sum of individual attribute values.

Tier 1							
Attribute Count	Attributes	Value	Victims	x	y		
1	Male	0.13	4	-80.59258	40.39013		
2	Adult	0.13	12	-80.06405	40.48027		
3	Decapitation	0.13	13	-80.06382	40.48000		
4	Mutilation	0.50					
5	Nude	0.29					
6	Dump Site	0.13					
7	Unhidden	0.13					
Attribute Score	Value Weight	Victim Score	Disparity Score	Final Score	Validity	Points	Ranking	Test
0.700	1.449	0.200	0.500	0.111	0.611	1.223	1.834	0.611

Victim Score: the ratio of victim output specific to the phenomenon (attribute filter combination) over the total number of victims possible. The output of victims divided by the total victims equals the victim score. The lower the victim score, the more conservative or specific the results (interpreted and ranked in tiers). This means that the lower the score is, the more significant the correlation between phenomenon and output (victims). However, this number means nothing without an attribute score to compare it against. The equation is the count of filtered attributes divided by the number of total attributes; from this a *disparity score* can be calculated by subtracting the attribute score from the victim score.

Disparity Score: the value that indicates the degree to which a tier can be considered liberal or conservative.

Final Score: takes into account all of the equation results and standardizes them by injecting a mathematical reconfiguration while retaining proportionality. This process also aids to produce values that do not skew the representation of information by inflating or deflating the scale when visually represented. It is of extreme importance to any statistical model to visualize the data on an equal plane so as not to bolster unintentional biases. This type of manipulation of descriptive statistics has been used to tip the table in favor of one argument or the other by projecting findings using a disproportionate scale relative to the values of the output. The final score is calculated as [(Value Weight × Disparity Score) / (Attribute Score − Victim Score)] / 13.

Validity: combines the disparity and final score to show overall significance.

Total Points: combines the disparity, final, and validity score to give a ranking.

Ranking: the higher the ranking number is, the higher is the probability for showing that a particular tier was significant in two ways: a large disparity score (large/small) and a final score that shows us how attribute score, value weight, victim score, and disparity score interact to create a ranking.

Now that the data has been normalized based on key attributes, we can set a critical level for the ranking scores and create validity based on points accumulated and arrange tiers based on this score. As a test, the ranking is subtracted from points and compared against validity, a process that should produce an identical number.

Each tier is evaluated and disqualified in three stages. Firstly, if the disparity score is either a negative number or a value below twenty-five (critical value), then it is disqualified. Secondly, if the attribute score is below fifty, it is disqualified. Finally, if the victim score is less than two, it is disqualified.

RANDOM TIERS

Random tiers were used to check the efficacy of the nonrandom tiers. This was accomplished by replicating each of the thirteen tiers by substituting random variables (attributes) using the *randbetween* function mentioned earlier. The two sets of tiers were constructed to mirror each other. Therefore if *nonrandom* tier number three had five attributes, *random* tier number three will also have five attributes designated.

In cases where the attribute score and the disparity score have the same value, the entire tier is unusable. It means that, given the combined attributes for the filter phenomenon, no outputs were returned because the filter combination did not identify links. This is the first metric looked at when assessing the validity of random tiers.

GEOGRAPHY

It should be noted that the following study is not a geographic profile because there simply are not enough data to evaluate and too many unknown or null data.

When looking at geography to assess spatial statistics, several important functions exist that allow for the analysis of patterns, clusters, and geographic distributions. By observing the outputs of the spatial analysis, we can then implement a *distance decay* function that is best suited for the phenomenon witnessed.[2] From this information, we can assign suspect ranking in relation to crime scenes and anchor points for both the suspects and the victims/crime scenes. In addition, we can use road networks to look at the most direct routes to and from crime scenes to anchor points, as well as to consider the adjacent topology, such as bridges, rail lines, or highways, that could factor into cost. From this information, we can deduce the suspects' awareness, activity, opportunity space, and buffer zone.[3] Because a geographic profile cannot be conducted on the Murder Swamp series, profiling methods will not be discussed here. The only aspects that remain pertinent are the concepts of *marauder* versus *commuter* serial criminals.

The phenomenon of commuter offenders, those who travel outside of their activity space to commit crime, is recent. It arose in America in the 1950s, with the advent of powerful cars and cheap gas. Law enforcement awareness of the commuter serial criminal grew in the 1970s, with the crime series of Henry Lee Lucas and Ted Bundy.

We must remember that although such instances were rare, there have been instances of violent serial offenders operating in relatively close proximity at the same time, and more than once law enforcement has attributed the victims of one offender to another offender. The murders committed by Herbert Mullin and Edmund Kemper in the area of Santa Cruz, California, by the Highway Killer and the Hillside Stranglers in the

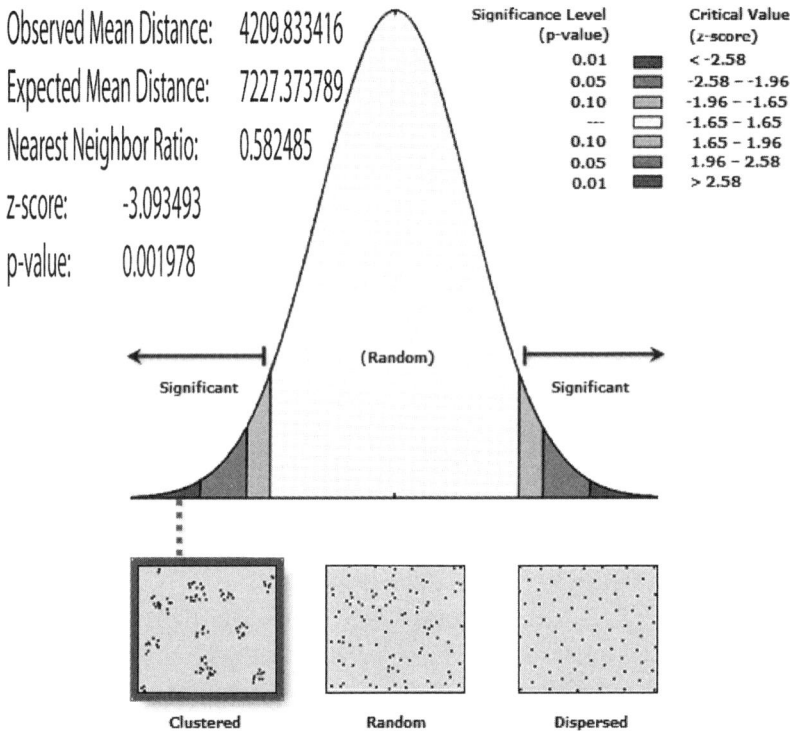

Figure 6. Average Nearest Neighbor Result

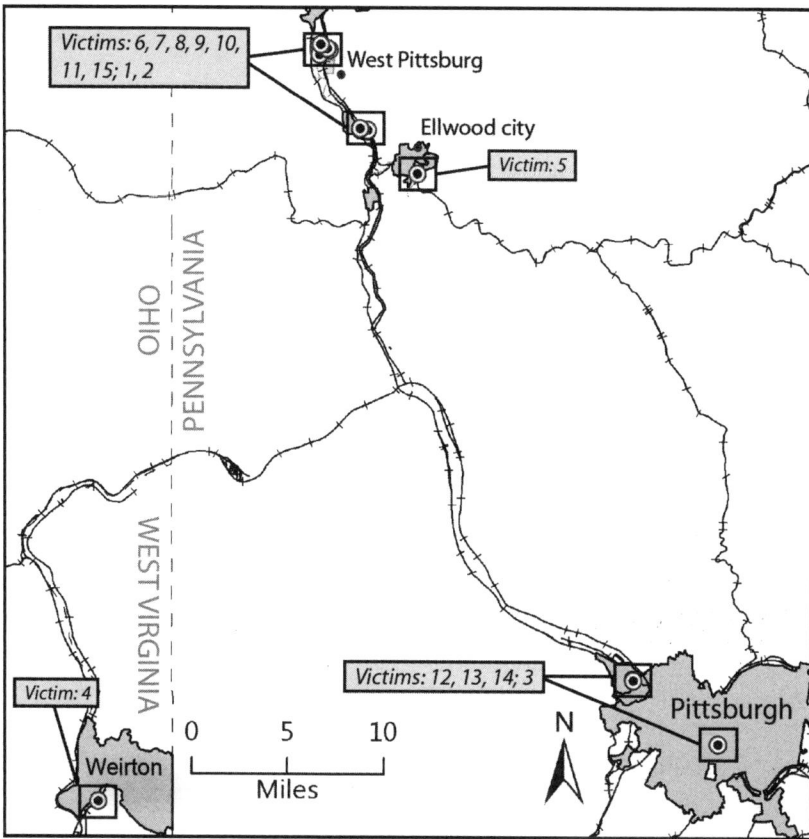

Figure 7. All Victims

area of Los Angeles, California, and by the Baseline Killer and the Phoenix Serial Shooter in Arizona are cases in point.

The temporal and geographic relationship shared by the Murder Swamp and Cleveland Torso series is tantalizing but not unique. Evaluated further, the modes of operation and ritualistic behavior displayed in these two series are distinctively different, as Badal has explained earlier in this book. Even in light of the fact that offenders' modes of operation are dynamic and ritualistic behavior is static, we know from criminological research that an offender may not display ritualistic behavior at a scene, for a variety of reasons already discussed. The crime scenes of the Murder Swamp series were in isolated areas sequestered from the greater population. Based on the *estimated* locations of victims' bodies, they are significantly clustered at P=.0019 Z=-3.09 (figures 6 and 7).

These victims were sequestered in an area that required the killer to have the knowledge and skills to traverse a treacherous terrain.

The Cleveland Torso victims, however, were statistically random (neither clustered nor random overall) at P=.025 Z=-1.88. They were in dispersed, unsequestered areas, and, more times than not, the killer made no attempt to conceal the crime.

FINDINGS AND CONCLUSION

The three victims discovered in boxcars shared some similar attributes, but there is not enough evidence to surmise that the same offender is responsible for all three killings. As noted earlier, staging is part of a killer's MO, who uses it to complete a crime successfully by avoiding apprehension. Posing is something much different; it is ritualistic and may be part of the offender's signature. Of the three boxcar victims, two were distinctively posed and killed elsewhere. The third boxcar victim was not posed, however, but was killed in place and had a word carved into his chest. Although this could be considered staging, there is really no way to tell if the perpetrator responsible for the first two victims was also responsible for the last. The first two victims of the boxcar killings definitely were posed, however, and, based on this analysis, these two victims are two of the three victims that could be considered to have been dispatched by the Cleveland Butcher.

So what do we know about the Butcher? Well, we know that the offender decapitated and mutilated his or her victims; we know that the perpetrator preferred dump sites as opposed to kill sites; and we know that the victims were posed and not concealed. Moreover, a recent geographic profile of the Cleveland Torso series identified the offender as a marauder rather then a commuter criminal. The Cleveland Butcher took care to clean the bodies, although whether the motivation was to wash away evidence or as part of ritualistic behavior is unknown. We do know someone taunted law enforcement and was strongly considered as a suspect in the killings. The Butcher was intimately acquainted with Cleveland and particularly Kingsbury Run, leaving the victims within his or her activity space to be discovered by an unfortunate fellow.

The Butcher exhibited the characteristics of an organized, power/control, hedonistic thrill killer, a conclusion based roughly on the revised

Holmes typology (Lester 1995, 80). A killer can appear to become disorganized without actually being so. However, an organized offender can have comorbid neuropathology, such as paranoid schizophrenia, that might further detract from his or her rationale, forcing the mutation from organized to disorganized. In summary, even when a killer is classified as an organized offender, situations can alter the typology to where the offender crosses into the spectrum of a mixed or disorganized offender.[4]

We also know that water played some part in the Butcher's killings, an attribute that may be part of the MO, used as a quick way to dispose of a body. We do not know, however, whether the Butcher cleaned the bodies found in water before dumping them there. The cleaning of a body is very intimate and fulfills a power/control model that is the overlying motivation for this type of offender. It is also important to note that the Butcher

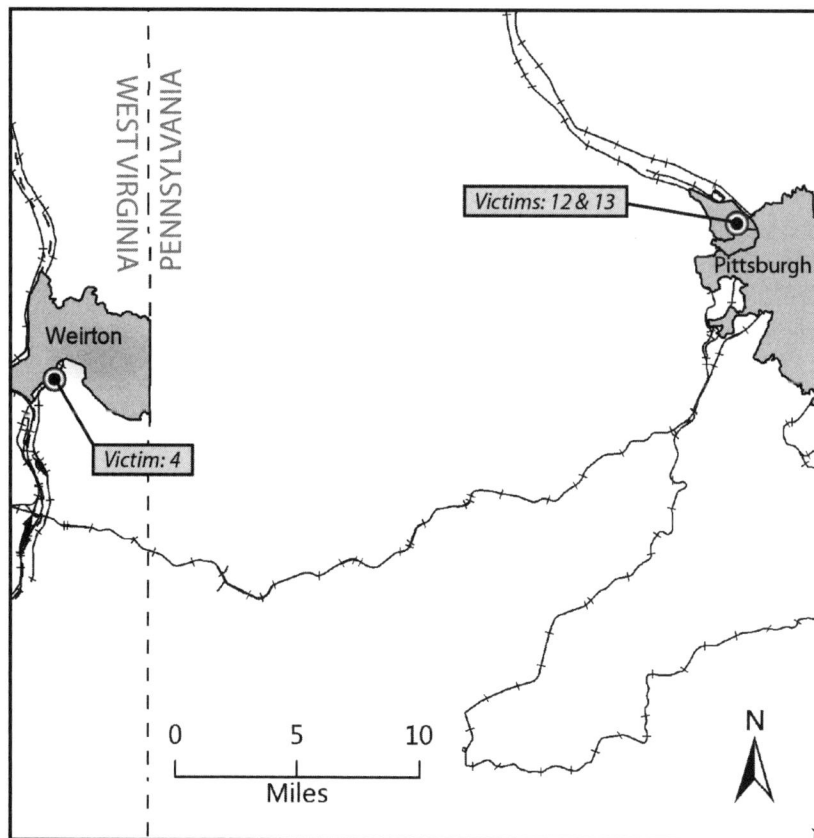

Figure 8. Victims 4, 12, and 13

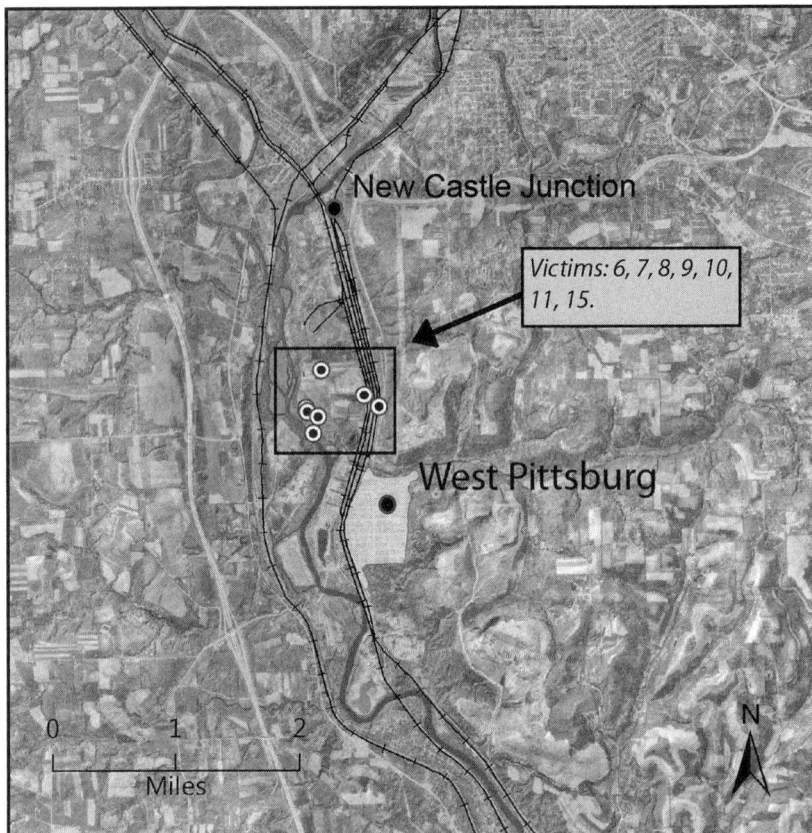

Figure 9. Victims near West Pittsburg

did not burn or set fire to the victims; instead—a fact that has been widely misinterpreted—the Butcher used chemical agents in order to preserve the body and did not intend to hide the crime. This is a fact that must not be overlooked: at no point did the Butcher attempt to completely sequester the evidence of his or her predatory dealings. Just as it is not unheard of for two serial killers to operate during the same period and in the same area, so it is likewise not unknown for a killer to stop killing for a significant period—because of incarceration, military service, or even (as in the case of Dennis Rader, the BTK killer), employment in a job giving the killer a measure of power over others. Killers know what they are doing, and they know what they are doing is wrong. The reader must understand that serial killers do not need a precipitating event to commit a crime. Such killers do not have a switch that turns on at random, compelling them to indulge in their aberrant behavior; as criminologist Jack Levin would say, "they are more bad than mad," and "their actions are sickening but they are not sick" (quoted in Meyer 2009). Given these facts, the idea that the Butcher might have taken an extended hiatus from killing should not be ruled out. Although we have learned a lot about the psychopathology of the serial killer, there is at least an equal amount that we still do not understand.

The attribute of posing was not employed with all of the Butcher's victims, but it is interesting in that it was employed with victims 12 and 13. It should be kept in mind that filters are based on evidence that is known and the final filter models do not include null values or those that were previously disqualified. Although it is interesting and logical that victims 4, 12, and 13 (figure 8) share the same correlation linkage—in fact, they share the majority of attributes that are consistent of what we know of the Butcher—this may be merely because we know more details of these victims than we do of the others.

Although most of the debate on this subject is focused around the victims found near West Pittsburg (figure 9), these victims are in fact those we should consider least when trying to understand and, if we can, link this horrendous series of events to the Mad Butcher of Kingsbury Run.

In the end we will never know unequivocally who the killer or killers were in either series of murders. What we do know from empirical analysis is that it is highly unlikely that the same offender, or offenders, were responsible for both the Cleveland Torso and Murder Swamp series. What we can say is that this model has shown that the highest correlation linkage exists among victims 4, 12, and 13 and that, based on the information available at this time, these are the only victims that can by any means be attributed to the Cleveland Butcher.

NOTES

1. For more information, see "GeoProfile: Developing an Establishing the Reliability of a New Geographic Profiling Software System," by Wesley English (English 2008); "The Microspatial Analysis of Crime," by Paul J. Brantingham (Brantingham and Brantingham 1984); *Crimestat: A Spatial Statistics Program for the Analysis of Crime* by Ned Levine (Levine 2004); and "Improving Geographic Profiling through Commuter/Marauder Prediction," by Derek Paulsen (Paulsen 2007).

2. For a complete list of distance decay functions and geographic profiling theory, see "GeoProfile: Developing an Establishing the Reliability of a New Geographic Profiling Software System," by Wesley English (English 2008).

3. For more information on geographic spaces, see "Wesley English, M.A., A Professional Profile," by Wesley English (English 2011).

4. For detailed information of the various typologies, see *Serial Killers: The Insatiable Passion,* by David Lester (Lester 1995, 70–84).

WORKS CITED

America's Serial Killers: Portraits in Evil. 2009. DVD. TV series directed by Ron Meyer. Golden Valley, Minn.: Mill Creek Entertainment.

Badal, James Jessen. 2001. *In the Wake of the Butcher: Cleveland's Torso Murders.* Kent: Kent State Univ. Press.

———. 2010. *Though Murder Has No Tongue: The Lost Victim of Cleveland's Mad Butcher.* Kent: Kent State Univ. Press.

Brantingham, Paul J. 1984. "The Microspatial Analysis of Crime." In *Patterns in Crime,* by Paul J. Brantingham and Patricia L. Brantingham, 322–65. New York: Collier Macmillan.

English, Wesley. 2008. "GeoProfile: Developing an Establishing the Reliability of a New Geographic Profiling Software System." Master's thesis, Chicago School of Professional Psychology.

———. 2011. "Wesley English, M.A., A Professional Profile." http://www.wesley-english.com/geoprofile.

The Fourteenth Victim: Elliot Ness and the Torso Murders. 2006. DVD. Documentary directed by Mark Wade Stone. Performed by Mark Wade Stone and James Jessen Badal. Lakewood, Ohio: Storytellers Media Group.

Kennedy, Leslie W., and Erin G. Van Brunschot. 2009. *The Risk in Crime.* Lanham, Md.: Rowman and Littlefield Publishers.

Keppel, Robert D., and William J. Birnes. 1997. *Signature Killers: Interpreting the Calling Cards of the Serial Murderer.* New York: Pocket Books.

Lester, David. 1995. *Serial Killers: The Insatiable Passion.* Philadelphia: Charles Press.

Levine, Ned. 2004. *Crimestat: A Spatial Statistics Program for the Analysis of Crime.* Washington, D.C.: National Institute of Justice.

Paulsen, Derek. 2007. "Improving Geographic Profiling through Commuter/Marauder Prediction." *Police Practice and Research* 8, no. 4 (September): 347–57.

BIBLIOGRAPHY

Allegheny County, Pa., Office of the Coroner. 1923. Cases C-165-23 (Charles McGregor), Oct. 3. Coroner's Office Records, 1884–1976. AIS.1982.07, Archives Service Center, University of Pittsburgh. Files include autopsy protocols, affidavits, police reports, and various pieces of official correspondence.

———. 1940. Cases C-40-34, C-40-35, C-40-36 (James Nicholson), May 3. Coroner's Office Records, 1884–1976. AIS.1982.07, Archives Service Center, University of Pittsburgh.

———. 1941. Unnumbered case (Wallace L. Brown), Sept. 24. Coroner's Office Records, 1884–1976. AIS.1982.07, Archives Service Center, University of Pittsburgh.

———. 1942. Cases C-42-57 (Ernest Alonzo), June 23. Coroner's Office Records, 1884–1976. AIS.1982.07, Archives Service Center, University of Pittsburgh.

Badal, James Jessen. 2001. *In the Wake of the Butcher: Cleveland's Torso Murders.* Kent, Ohio: Kent State Univ. Press.

———. 2010. *Though Murder Has No Tongue: The Lost Victim of Cleveland's Mad Butcher.* Kent, Ohio: Kent State Univ. Press.

"The Black Hand." 2010. GangRule.com: A Look at the Emergence of the New York Mafia Through 1900–1920. http://www.gangrule.com/gangs/the-black-hand. Dec. 6.

Gilmore, John. 2006. *Severed: The True Story of the Black Dahlia Murder.* 2nd ed. Los Angeles, Calif.: Amok Books.

Johnson, Paul G. 2007. "Murder Swamp." Unpublished manuscript. Private collection of Paul Johnson.

———. N.d. Newspaper clippings, source unknown. Private collection of Paul Johnson.

Lawrence County Historical Society. 2010. "The Black Hand." Lawrence County Historical Society, http://www.lawrencechs.com/museum/collections/the-black-hand/.

Martin, John Bartlow. 1949. "Butcher's Dozen: The Cleveland Torso Murders." *Harper's Magazine,* November.

McClung, Paul. 1952. "The Fiend Has a Thousand Eyes." *Front Page Detective,* July.

Merylo, Peter. Daily police reports, 1936–44. Private Collection of Merylo Family.

———. N.d. Papers. Private Collection of Merylo Family.

———. N.d. Unpublished memoir. Private Collection of Merylo Family.

———, and Frank Otwell. N.d. Unpublished memoir. Private Collection of Merylo Family.

Ove, Torsten. 2000. "Mafia Has Long History Here, Growing from Bootlegging Days." *Pittsburgh Post-Gazette,* Nov. 6. Post-gazette.com. http://old.post-gazette.com/regionstate/20001106mobhistory2.asp (accessed Dec. 6, 2010).

CONTEMPORARY NEWSPAPERS, WITH DATES

Cleveland News. Oct. 14, 1939; May 3–4, 17, 1940.

Cleveland Plain Dealer. May 4, 1940.

Cleveland Press. Oct. 14, 19, 1939; May 3–4, 1940.

East Liverpool [Ohio] Evening Review. Feb. 12–13, 19, 1924.

New Castle Herald. Mar. 17–18, 1921.

New Castle News. July 11, Oct. 6, 1923; Jan. 3–8, Oct. 6–10, 14, 19–21, 1925; July 2, 1936; Oct. 16–17, 19–20, 1939; May 3, Nov. 2, 4, 1940.

Pittsburgh Post-Gazette. Oct. 6–7, 1923; May 4–6, 1940.

Pittsburgh Press. Oct. 3, 1923; May 3–4, 1940; June 1, Sept. 24, 1941; June 23–24, 1942.

Pittsburgh Sun Telegraph. May 3–5, 1940; May 26, 31, Sept. 25, 1941; June 22, 1942.

Steubenville [Ohio] *Herald Star.* Feb. 12–15, 1924.

Youngstown Vindicator. May 3–4, 8, 1940.

INDEX